eBay
Rescue

Profit
Maker

Kevin W. Boyd

FEB - - 2009

ALPHA

A member of Penguin Group (USA) Inc.

DU

ALPHA BOOKS

Published by the Penguin Group

Penguin Group (USA) Inc., 375 Hudson Street, New York, New York 10014, USA

Penguin Group (Canada), 90 Eglinton Avenue East, Suite 700, Toronto, Ontario M4P 2Y3, Canada (a division of Pearson Penguin Canada Inc.)

Penguin Books Ltd., 80 Strand, London WC2R 0RL, England

Penguin Ireland, 25 St. Stephen's Green, Dublin 2, Ireland (a division of Penguin Books Ltd.)

Penguin Group (Australia), 250 Camberwell Road, Camberwell, Victoria 3124, Australia (a division of Pearson Australia Group Pty. Ltd.)

Penguin Books India Pvt. Ltd., 11 Community Centre, Panchsheel Park, New Delhi—110 017, India

Penguin Group (NZ), 67 Apollo Drive, Rosedale, North Shore, Auckland 1311, New Zealand (a division of Pearson New Zealand Ltd.)

Penguin Books (South Africa) (Pty.) Ltd., 24 Sturdee Avenue, Rosebank, Johannesburg 2196, South Africa

Penguin Books Ltd., Registered Offices: 80 Strand, London WC2R 0RL, England

Copyright © 2009 by Kevin W. Boyd

International Standard Book Number: 978-1-59257-809-2
Library of Congress Catalog Card Number: 2008931264

11 10 09   8 7 6 5 4 3 2 1

Interpretation of the printing code: The rightmost number of the first series of numbers is the year of the book's printing; the rightmost number of the second series of numbers is the number of the book's printing. For example, a printing code of 09-1 shows that the first printing occurred in 2009.

Printed in the United States of America

Note: This publication contains the opinions and ideas of its author. It is intended to provide helpful and informative material on the subject matter covered. It is sold with the understanding that the author and publisher are not engaged in rendering professional services in the book. If the reader requires personal assistance or advice, a competent professional should be consulted.

The author and publisher specifically disclaim any responsibility for any liability, loss, or risk, personal or otherwise, which is incurred as a consequence, directly or indirectly, of the use and application of any of the contents of this book.

Trademarks: All terms mentioned in this book that are known to be or are suspected of being trademarks or service marks have been appropriately capitalized. Alpha Books and Penguin Group (USA) Inc. cannot attest to the accuracy of this information. Use of a term in this book should not be regarded as affecting the validity of any trademark or service mark.

Most Alpha books are available at special quantity discounts for bulk purchases for sales promotions, premiums, fund-raising, or educational use. Special books, or book excerpts, can also be created to fit specific needs.

For details, write: Special Markets, Alpha Books, 375 Hudson Street, New York, NY 10014.

Publisher: Marie Butler-Knight

Editorial Director: Mike Sanders

Senior Managing Editor: Billy Fields

Acquisitions Editor: Tom Stevens

Development Editor: Nancy D. Lewis

Production Editor: Kayla Dugger

Copy Editor: Amy Lepore

Cover & Book Designer: Kurt Owens

Indexer: Brad Herriman

Layout: Brian Massey

Proofreader: Laura Caddell

Contents

Introduction

This book contains information that will change your thinking about your own eBay business. You'll progress from your current questions, possible frustration, and discouragement to solutions and discover a product selection and selling methodology that actually works. The **SEE ALSO** entries will point you to sections of a chapter or appendix for more in-depth information about a related subject.

I have invested too much time learning, and then refining, these methods not to share this information. Included are worksheets with step-by-step instructions that you will use to generate your product ideas and determine which of these products are profitable. Strategies and recommended tools are provided specifically to help you locate reputable suppliers and create professional-quality listings that will sell your products.

You will need to download and print the worksheets and other forms used in this book. There is no charge for the download at www. trainingu4auctions.com/notebook.

If you are wondering, "Will these methodologies actually work for me? Can I really start, grow, and run a profitable eBay business?" Consider this ...

"If you think you can, or think you can't, you are right!"
—Henry Ford

Fear of failure is normal. To win at anything you have to overcome your fears and then get in the game. Most eBay sellers are just like you. Anyone can sell on eBay. But the successful ones become motivated enough to learn how to sell properly and profitably. Challenge yourself and decide to join the eBay profit makers!

Acknowledgments

I acknowledge and sincerely thank the publisher and the creative and knowledgeable editors that made this book possible. A special thank you to Tom Stevens, Lissa McGrath, Kayla Dugger, Amy Lepore, and Nancy Lewis.

Trademarks

Where Are My Profits?

Many eBay sellers begin their new venture with excitement. At first they have high expectations and energy. They may list many items but, over time, realize that their listings are producing hit-or-miss results. After several more months of less-than-expected results, their enthusiasm begins to fade. They continue selling the same items with disappointing results until one day they conclude, "You can't make any money on eBay." Then sadly they quit. Who do they blame? eBay.

Unfortunately, what these sellers don't realize is that success could actually be just around the corner. The problem is that they can't seem to ever get around that corner. They are walking in place and don't know how to move forward. The reason is simple—they keep making the same mistakes over and over again. I can relate.

As an active and experienced eBay seller for many years now, I have certainly made my share of mistakes along the way. I was determined, however, to make eBay work for me. Eventually and fortunately, I discovered what I was doing wrong. Over time, I have developed and refined my own methodology for eBay marketplace analysis that uncovers only profitable products.

Now, as an eBay instructor and consultant, I continue to see many eBay sellers making the same mistakes I did when I started. Actual profit (not just sales) for many eBay sellers remains elusive. I realized that eBay sellers needed a solid methodology and support system that cuts through the hype, avoids the traps, and finds profitable products. The desire to share my solution with struggling eBay sellers was the inspiration for this book.

The #1 Mistake New eBay Sellers Make

I was reminded during a recent consultation with one of my clients that nearly all new eBay sellers make a certain mistake. I made this mistake when I first started my eBay venture, and maybe you have made it as well. It is a costly mistake that, if not stopped, is the fastest way to eBay ruin.

Question: What is the #1 mistake new eBay sellers make?

Answer: They purchase items to sell on eBay based on one reason— the items are "cheap!"

Buying items simply because they are cheap is no guarantee that you can actually make any money when selling them. Many new eBay sellers buy several cheap items and are all excited about the discounted prices. Maybe they find a liquidation sale and pick up a large quantity of the product. Many times they spend hundreds or even thousands of dollars for the merchandise.

Then they list one of the items on eBay. When the listing ends, they find to their dismay that their item sold for even less on eBay than what they had paid. Thinking it was a fluke, they adjust their listing in some way and try relisting it again. Same result. After a few more listings, they are faced with a sobering fact. Their product selection has resulted in a room (or garage) full of merchandise that will take them two years to sell, and every sale will be at a loss. Again, I can relate.

The eBay Rut

Another common problem for eBay sellers is what I call the "eBay rut." They view their gross sales as their metric for success. "Well, I sell over $1,000 each month and that makes me a PowerSeller!" Okay, your sales look great—how's your profit?

They have become so busy listing, selling, and shipping their products that they rarely pause to see just how profitable their sales are. When they look at their PayPal account at the end of the month, they see that it has not increased. Yet they continue selling the same items month after month, sometimes year after year. These sellers do not have a business, they have a shipping hobby.

Other sellers seem to be motivated only to collect positive feedback. "Wow, I just reached 500 feedbacks, and all are 100 percent positive!"

Congratulations! That is truly an important achievement. Your feedback looks great—how's your profit?

If your eBay selling is more a fun hobby, then have fun. Nevertheless, even hobbyist sellers should consider what their benefit is from all of the effort required to list, sell, pack, and ship their products each month. Their primary goal should be profit.

The Root Problem

For some sellers, unfortunately, their profitability problem is never resolved because they do not understand the root cause. Many think that they just need to change the keywords, use a different listing format, insert more pictures, or write a better description. While tweaking a listing in order to increase the number of bids is important, it does not address the root problem.

Their problem is simply this—they are selling the wrong products on eBay. Fine-tuning a listing will not solve the problem of limited demand or too much competition. The products will remain unprofitable.

Imagine that you have decided to open a shoe store in a new strip mall. You didn't check the location. You just signed the lease, ordered your products, and are now ready for the sales to roll in. Then you discover that of the 20 stores in the mall, every one of them is also a shoe store selling the same shoes you are. How well do you think you will do?

This problem could have been avoided if only you had checked to see what your competition would be before you decided to sell shoes in that mall. What you should have done instead is open a store that sells very popular products that no other store at that mall sells. In short, you want products with high demand and low competition.

While that example may seem obvious, the vast majority of eBay sellers are in fact doing the very same thing. They never check out the demand, competition, or profitability of the products before they purchase them for resale. "Look, here is a cheap, cool, fun, or unusual product. Let's try selling this one!" So they list it on eBay and cross their fingers. There is no proven method to their product selection decision making. That is the root problem.

Question: What do you call a fun hit-or-miss hobby that involves winning or losing money?

Answer: Gambling!

Stop spinning the eBay product roulette wheel and start selling "sure things." Choose products with high demand, low competition, and that are proven profitable on eBay.

Reality Check: How Is Your eBay Business Doing?

Are you making random product selections that produce disappointing results? Is there no proven method to your product choices? These mistakes happened to me as well when I was a beginning seller. After a few costly stumbles early on, I quickly realized my mistakes and, for the most part, have not made them again. My turnaround happened immediately when I stopped treating my eBay selling as just a "fun hit-or-miss hobby" and started treating it like a serious business.

New sellers tend to think of the fun instead of the profit. Be careful because that is a very quick path to your new eBay venture's exit strategy.

The most important metric for any business, including eBay selling, is profit. Without profit, you are doing volunteer work just to ship products at or below the cost to your customers.

Before you decide which products you will sell on eBay:

- Do you have a methodology for your product selection process that has proven successful?
- Do you conduct eBay marketplace analysis?
- Is there market demand for your products?
- Have you checked your competition?
- Do you know what the chances are that the products will sell?
- Do you know what price the item is selling for on eBay?
- Will your item be profitable?

If you have answered "no" to most of these questions, you have just discovered the root cause of your profitability problem. The solution is to approach your product selection and sourcing like a businessperson.

Have you ever wondered, "Just what do eBay professionals know that I don't?" The answer is probably quite a bit if you are new to eBay or your business is not yet thriving. Some professionals have been self-taught through trial and error, but all have become successful because, at some point in time, they finally stopped treating their product selection haphazardly. They now approach their sales on eBay like a conventional business with proven methodologies for marketplace analysis, product selection, inventory management, and positive growth.

As you progress through this book, I will present my proven product selection methodologies using a series of steps and decision-making worksheets. Learning and then following these methodologies will develop and implement your eBay business plan for success. The tough work is already done for you. All you will need to do is take action and follow the methodology.

Chart Your Roadmap to eBay Success

Have you developed a plan for your eBay business? If you become bored with even the thought of this subject, consider how important this question is to your success.

I am not asking you to develop a detailed business plan complete with projected profit and loss statements. However, you need to chart your roadmap. Without it, you don't know where you are going, much less how to get there.

Spend some time thinking about the following critical success factors for your eBay business. Write your initial thoughts and ideas in the space provided here. As you progress through the book, you will modify and refine your plans. If you need more space than is provided, you can download these questions in a PDF file for printing at www. trainingu4auctions.com/notebook.

Why do you want to sell on eBay?

To get rid of stuff, as a hobby, financial reasons, easiest entry to online selling, part-time income, full-time income?

_____

_____

_____

_____

_____

_____

What will be your sales channels?

EBay, other online sites, your own website, fairs, trade shows, consignment stores?

_____

_____

_____

Where will your business be located?

Home-based business, established business, industrial park?

_____

How will you fund your business?

Savings, loans, partners, other?

_____

_____

What will you sell?

New products, used products, services, a combination?

_____

_____

Where will you get your products?

Estate sales, liquidators, wholesalers, drop shippers, importers, surplus, other auction sites, other?

_____

_____

_____

_____

_____

Where will you store your products?

Home, garage, rental unit, industrial park?

_____

How will you market your business?

EBay only, off eBay, trade shows, promotional flyers, newsletters, discussion boards, other?

_____

_____

_____

_____

What will be your costs?

Fixed, variable, product (cost of goods sold [COGS]), eBay and PayPal fees, other?

_____

_____

_____

_____

_____

How do you define success?

Financial, sales volume, profit, establish a business, become a
PowerSeller, provide supplemental part-time or full-time income?
Develop a checklist known only to you with immediate and future
goals and accomplishments.

_____

_____

_____

_____

How will you measure success?

Determine your annual, quarterly, and monthly sales and financial
goals and metrics.

_____

_____

_____

_____

_____

When will you be profitable?

One month, six months, one year, three years, ever?

_____

_____

Spend some time developing your answers to these questions. As you
progress through this book, revisit these questions periodically.
Expect that some of your initial answers will need to be changed.
Welcome this, for it shows that the methodology is working. Thought-
ful answers to these questions will provide the proper mindset to
develop and then refine your own roadmap for success.

A Positive Marketing Mindset

Can a positive attitude affect profit? Most MBAs and CPAs would say "no." I tend to disagree with them. A positive attitude will certainly keep you motivated through the tough times. The most powerful formula for success, though, is when you combine a positive attitude with the right mindset and specific knowledge.

In this chapter, you will learn the advantages and disadvantages of selling in different markets. This discussion is not meant to discourage or sidetrack you. On the contrary, it will enable you to thoroughly understand what not to sell, what selling phase your business is in, what niches to choose, and how competition affects you. Adjusting your mindset will help replace the old attitudes of product selection with new possibilities and fresh ideas for undiscovered markets.

The eBay Selling Progression

Serious eBay sellers usually pass through three distinct phases: beginner, advanced, and professional. Note that "beginner" does not mean you are only getting rid of stuff around the house. It means you are in the beginning phase of an eBay business.

Determine which phase you are in currently and then which one you want to attain. Study the following "best practice" selling strategies that serious sellers should use for each phase.

Phase I—Beginner

Avoid lower-priced items:

- It takes just as long to pack and ship a $5 item as it does a $50 item. It is usually not worth the effort to list, sell, pack, and ship individual items that are less than $10 or $20. The exception to this rule is a bait product.

SEE ALSO **Chapter 9, "Determine Your Bait Products"**

- Sell items priced between $20 and $100. You want volume more than value because of common mistakes beginners will make. Move into Phase II as soon as possible.

Conduct eBay market research:

- Study the top sellers of the items you sell before you create your listings. Mimic how they list their items, and you can expect the same results.

Create appealing listings:

- Create listings that will generate the most hits and bring the highest bids.

SEE ALSO **Chapter 7, "Create Professional Listings"**

- Learn how to take professional-looking photos.

Pack items properly and ship quickly:

- The first impression of your customer service is the way you ship the product.
- Use boxes specifically designed for shipping that are suitable for the item's dimensions and weight.
- Use sufficient packing material to protect the item during transit.
- Ship as soon as possible using the carrier and services most appropriate and practical for the item.

SEE ALSO **Chapter 8, "Ship Quickly"**

Phase II—Advanced

Sell medium- to higher-priced items:

- Sell items to individuals in the $50 to $200 range.
- Sell higher-priced items ($200 to $2,000) to businesses. Think higher-priced items and higher volume.

- Strive to attain PowerSeller status through higher sales levels and superior customer service and satisfaction.

- Use product sourcing and analysis tools to find products and know that they are profitable.

- Source your products from reputable liquidators, wholesalers, and drop shippers. Expand with new products into new niches and categories.

Use advanced listing strategies:

- Use bulk-listing tools such as Turbo Lister to more efficiently create listings.

- Distinguish yourself from your competition with effective use of subtitles, different gallery photos, and listing upgrades.

- Purchase quality photography equipment.

- Open an eBay Store. Cross-promote your store items with related standard listings.

- Consider selling internationally.

Sell in "lots":

- Sell items in quantity using Fixed Price listings.

- Group multiple different-but-related items in one listing.

Manage your product line and inventory wisely:

- Spread your money wide and thin among many different products rather than narrow and deep among just a few.

- Eliminate nonprofitable inventory. Add new products and new niches. Always be looking for new, profitable products.

Phase III—Professional

Sell higher-priced, higher-profit items:

- Sell items $100+ to individuals and $500 to $10,000 to businesses. You want higher-priced, higher-profit, medium-volume items with little competition and high demand.

- Sell in the Business and Industrial categories.

- Purchase in bulk to receive greater volume discounts. Consider buying from importers. Consider becoming an importer.

- Use different sales channels such as trade shows and other online auction sites. Consider opening your own website.

What Not to Sell

Before we begin a discussion on what you should sell, let's first trim back your search. You need to understand the items that you should not sell because of typically poor results. There are also many products that are either restricted or not allowed on eBay.

Prohibited and Restricted Items

EBay has strict rules for what items are allowed, prohibited, or restricted. If you think of products that are highly regulated by the government, you can quickly identify items that are potential violations. Anything related to weapons, alcohol, tobacco, pornography, drugs, medical devices, intellectual property (copyright, patent, or trademark infringement), and items from countries that the United States does not trade with (such as Cuba) are just a few examples of items that are either prohibited or restricted.

As the seller, it is your responsibility to understand and not violate these rules and policies. EBay has sophisticated software applications that constantly scour all eBay listings searching for violators. If you are caught selling these items, your listing will be cancelled, and you will forfeit your eBay listing fees. A severe or unlawful violation, such as selling Cuban cigars, will most likely result in account suspension.

If you are thinking of selling any item that gives you even the slightest concern that it may violate eBay's rules, then be sure and be safe. Select the **Help** link at the top of any page and type **prohibited and restricted items** in the search field. If you are still unsure after reviewing eBay's policies for particular items, contact a live eBay representative. Go to eBay's homepage and select the **Live help** link at the top right of the screen. A window will open, and you can chat online with a live eBay representative. If the representative is not certain whether your item is allowed, he or she may have you forward your question to another eBay department.

Recalled Items

You are not allowed to sell any items that have been recalled by the U.S. Consumer Product Safety Commission (CPSC). It is your responsibility to ensure that your products have not been recalled. Claiming ignorance of this rule is not a defense, and violators will have their listings cancelled and possibly their eBay account suspended.

It seems that recalled items are in the news often. We are all familiar with the product recalls that resulted from lead paint used on toys made in China. If you sell toys, even used toys, you need to be sure they have not been recalled. There are many other products, however, that have been recalled that do not make the nightly news. In fact, it is surprising how many products that could be sold in several categories on eBay have actually been recalled.

It is a good idea for you to check the CPSC website every few weeks or whenever you are considering adding new items to your product line. You can search the CPSC recalled product list at www.cpsc.gov/cpscpub/prerel/prerel.html. New recalls are usually posted on the eBay Announcements board as well.

Difficult Products to Ship

It may be profitable selling large or heavy items, but then you have to ship them. Many times beginning eBay students tell me they just purchased a particular item to sell on eBay. Then their question to me is, "We had to haul it away in our truck. How should we ship it?" I would ask them, "Why did you buy something that big when you knew you would have to ship it?"

Consider the storage space needed for large items. Think of having to maneuver a sizeable item in your garage or later in your vehicle on the trip to your shipping carrier. Avoid oversized and heavy items unless you have a wholesaler drop ship for you (a wholesaler that will ship an item to your customer for you) or you have the facilities and a workforce to handle them. Sell only items that are easy to store, pack, and ship.

SEE ALSO **Chapter 10, "Are You Ready for Drop Shipping?"**

Products or Categories with Tough Competition

Let's face it, some of the categories on eBay are saturated. When you scroll page by page, you see the same products being sold by several sellers. Most importantly, you see that there are no bids. There is no reason to attempt to sell these products even if you have found a great deal. For some reason, many eBay sellers never realize this and continue trying to sell in a ridiculously crowded and competitive marketplace.

The good news is that eBay and other sources have excellent tools to show you congested categories before you even spend a dime. To quickly determine whether a category is saturated, click the **Advanced Search** link, type the keywords for the product you want to sell, and then click the checkbox **Completed listings only.** EBay will now return search results for all completed listings in the last two weeks on eBay that had the same keywords in their title.

Scroll through several pages looking at the price column. The prices that are in green mean that those items sold. Items with red prices indicate that those items did not sell. If you scroll through several pages and most of the listings for the product you want to sell are in red, forget about the product. It is not profitable on eBay and is not worth wasting another minute of your time.

Cheap Products

Don't sell items that are cheap in price or quality. If the items are cheap in quality, you are selling junk. Expect customer dissatisfaction, a lot of returns, and bad feedback. There is no reason to sell poor-quality items if you want to build a reputable eBay business.

I also suggest that you avoid selling items that are cheap in price. I try to draw the line at a $10 price tag. In fact, my recommended minimum is a $10 profit, not just price.

To be clear, I am not talking about minimum pricing when you are cleaning out your closet. When you just want to get rid of stuff, get rid of it. I am referring to your decision process when choosing the type of items that you will purchase to become part of your product line in your eBay business.

Selling individual items under $10 is, for the most part, too much effort for too little reward. How many $8 items ($5 profit) do you have to sell to make a profit of $1,000 a month on eBay? Answer: 200! That means 200 listings, 200 sales, 200 boxes to pack, and 200 shipments to prepare. Even if each one only takes a total of 10 minutes for the complete process, that is 2,000 minutes or over 33 hours.

Compare this to an advanced eBay seller who lists more valuable items in the $150 to $200 range for a $100 profit. She needs to sell just 10 items to make $1,000. It also takes her a little more than an hour and a half per month. The point here is that it takes just as long to list, pack, and ship an item with a $5 profit as it does an item with a $100 profit. Sell items that are worthy of your valuable time and effort.

New, Hot-Selling Consumer Electronics

I know consumer electronics are hip, trendy, glitzy, and irresistible to the many men who are eBay sellers. It is very cool to brag to your friends that you sell the latest electronic gadgets. You can ignore my advice and try to sell these items if you want, just don't expect to make any money on eBay. I can't be more blunt than that.

The consumer electronics industry is probably the most fiercely competitive marketplace. Look what happened to Good Guys, Ultimate Electronics, and even CompUSA to name a few. Even Circuit City struggles to compete with Best Buy.

You cannot compete with all these large corporations' purchasing power for new, state-of-the-art, mass-market consumer electronics. Most of the popular items are not even available to part-time sellers. You need a physical retail store with an enormous inventory investment and insurance policy. Even if you have a source for these items, you will be doing well just to break even on eBay.

Guys, sorry to disappoint you. Be glad that you have just saved yourself a lot of money, time, and effort. Now I have an alternative for you.

About the only way to profitably sell these types of mass-market items is to sell older model units or their accessories. Yes, there is a market on eBay for two- to three-year-old models of many items. You can purchase these products in hugely discounted liquidation sales (meaning discounted heavily off the wholesale price at pennies on the dollar) directly from the manufacturer or from various liquidation sites (see the section "Mass Market vs. Niche Market" later in this chapter).

Your Own Creations: Art, Photography, or Books

Unless you are a known celebrity or artist, it is very difficult to sell your own creations on eBay. Scrolling through these types of categories on eBay will reveal many items selling for less than $10, some as low as 99 cents. This breaks our rule for selling items under the $10 minimum profit threshold.

Many sellers have tried to sell their own handcrafted items on eBay with little success. I even know of one couple who both quit their jobs to build and sell bird feeders on eBay. Ironically, they had not sold even one bird feeder on eBay before they made that decision. They just thought it was a good idea and jumped off the cliff together. It nearly wiped them out financially while they struggled to find new jobs.

Unfortunately, the same poor sales record can be expected from your own artwork, photography, music, or writing. There is little demand on eBay for unknown artists. If I wanted a lot of nice but cheap artwork to decorate a model home, I would go to eBay. It is a great place to buy artwork, but most likely if you try to sell it you will be disappointed.

It is probably best when just starting to sell your own artwork, photography, or handcrafted items by renting a booth at fairs and trade shows. Then network and make important connections in your craft or industry to gain more exposure and market your work. Consider getting a website or using an eBay Store as your website and print the web address (URL) on your business cards. This way, interested customers or dealers can contact you or purchase your items after the show.

Always perform the "completed listings" research method previously described for the items you are thinking of selling. When you see a string of red prices, run away. Most importantly, don't quit your day job.

Unprofitable Products

If the product you want to sell is not profitable on eBay, why would you want to sell it? Many new sellers want to sell the latest gadgets and hottest items. Maybe they see something on store shelves, in magazines, or in other advertising and think, "Wow, that thing is hot.

I want to sell it on eBay." This is a natural and common first thought when considering what to sell. However, what is hot on store shelves is not always hot or profitable on eBay.

Most shoppers check eBay looking for items at a reduced price. They think of eBay as the outlet mall of the online world, and for the most part, they are right. Amateur sellers who have access to items that are hot on store shelves will often sell these items on eBay for no profit. They have no understanding of how retail selling works, and all they know to do is to keep lowering the price. I have even seen many items selling for less than what I know they must have paid. What is going on?

Could it be that these sellers know something you don't or have some secret access to wholesale products that you don't? Are they selling these items as a loss leader in order to interest the customer in an upgraded, higher-value product? Maybe, but in most cases no. These are simply amateur sellers who are losing money on each sale.

Don't jump into their crazy circus. It is a guaranteed losing proposition. They will not be around long, but meanwhile you cannot compete. What you must determine is what items are hot and profitable on eBay, not in stores. EBay is a completely different marketplace.

What You Should Sell

First and foremost, if you want to actually make money from your eBay sales, you must sell items that are profitable. While that seems like an obvious idea, you have read enough in this book so far to realize that it is not. The problem again is that many eBay sellers have no methodology to their product selection. Their decisions are based on hunches. They just guess with results that are hit and miss, and in many cases they miss by a mile. They have no idea how to determine what will be a winner on eBay.

Don't base your product selection on a hunch or guesswork. What you need is a proven methodology that, through the process of analysis and elimination, will sift out the losers and find your remaining gold nuggets.

General Market vs. Specialty Market

The first question you need to answer is, "What type of products do I want to sell, general products or specialty products?" Both methods can be successful on eBay, but each has certain advantages and disadvantages. Each method requires different sources of products and strategies of selling. As you progress and expand your eBay selling, you can certainly use both methods. For now, in order to keep from being overwhelmed, you want to narrow your focus to just one.

General Market Selling

General market refers to selling many different and unrelated items. There is no particular theme to your selling except that you want great products at great prices.

Think of Costco (or Sam's Club). What a cool store. I love going there to browse. It seems that every time I visit Costco they have fantastic new items that I have never seen before and at great prices. With my next visit, however, those items are often gone and usually are not found there again. Many times I have verbally kicked myself for not buying a particular item. The great prices, along with the anticipation I have for finding another terrific product, is what keeps me going back to Costco again and again.

If you want to generalize, that is what your model should be. You are constantly adding new products, and once they are gone, they are gone. Your satisfied customers will keep coming back looking for another great product that you may have listed. They will also sign up for your newsletter mailing list (if you have an eBay Store) and save you as one of their favorite sellers. You need to stock several varied products and then keep them fresh and moving.

The main source of products for general sales is usually liquidators, estate sales, government liquidation, surplus, or local businesses that want to get rid of items quickly. While all of these sources are legitimate, some are much more time-consuming than others.

Many of the items you will find in estate and garage sales will be used items, and much of it is junk. Traveling to all the weekend estate sales is a very time-consuming process that produces very few, if any, exceptional "finds." This is fine if you want to do this for fun, but your benefit-to-effort ratio will be quite low. If your eBay sales are more than a hobby, then it is much more efficient to look for your gold nuggets online.

Do not confuse online sources of liquidation and surplus items with junk. Manufacturers and large retail stores outsource the liquidation of their products when seasons or fashions change, new models replace older ones, or the items are slow moving. These businesses use reputable liquidators who purchase large quantities of the product (known as "lots") at enormous discounts and then sell them to other retailers or product suppliers for a markup. Liquidators make their profit from the sheer volume of product that moves through their giant warehouses.

The major advantage of sourcing general-item products is that you can pick up products for just a few cents on the retail dollar. You may find a product that sold for $100 retail for less than $5. This is significantly less than purchasing from wholesalers at only 45 to 50 percent off the retail price.

There are, however, at least two major disadvantages with general sales product sourcing. First, it is very time-consuming searching for items by attending local auctions, estate sales, and garage sales. Second, if you purchase items from liquidation sites, you usually have to purchase the complete lot. This means you may have to purchase 500 items sight-unseen, have them shipped to you by a major trucking line, and then have enough storage space. For the beginning eBay seller with no storage space, this means your cars are now in your driveway because your garage is now your warehouse.

There is another problem with using liquidators. Most liquidators are now using the Internet to sell their items. If you conducted an Internet search for "liquidators," you would receive thousands of hits. Here is the problem: who is reputable and who is not? If the source of your product will be liquidators, then you need some way to weed through and buy only from reputable liquidators.

SEE ALSO **Chapter 6, "Finding Reputable Suppliers"**

Specialty Market Selling

Specialty market selling involves products that have a common theme. When you specialize, you have narrowed your products to include only related items so that the clutter of unrelated items does not confuse your customers. Think of a specialty bead shop. It stocks everything related to the beading hobby. It does not stock lawnmower parts.

Most specialty sellers have an eBay Store to display all their items much like a website. Customers will come back because you sell quality products that they want more of or because they consume them and need more. They will also refer their friends to your store.

The biggest advantage of specialty selling is that, once you have a proven, profitable product line, you can keep relisting these same products over and over again. This is lower maintenance compared to general selling, in which you are constantly on the hunt for products. You will, of course, still need to add new products and drop poor-performing products. However, this is more of a quarterly chore if you are a specialty seller as compared to weekly when you general sell.

Another advantage is that, because you will be purchasing your products from wholesalers, you are more in control of your inventory. You do not have to purchase pallets of items because many wholesalers have much lower minimum order requirements. If you use drop shippers, you have virtually no inventory.

Two disadvantages occur when specialty selling. First, because you will purchase your products from wholesalers, you will need a business license before you can order from them. However, this a temporary disadvantage.

SEE ALSO **Chapter 12, "Get Your Business License"**

The second disadvantage is that you will be paying full wholesale prices for your items. Wholesale prices average about 40 to 50 percent off the retail price. While this may still seem to be a good discount, it is nowhere near the unit price you can achieve when purchasing liquidation items. In addition, you can't assume you will be able to sell these items at full retail price on eBay. You will need to compete with retailers and other online sites. You must provide something that your competition doesn't, and usually it is a lower price.

Another disadvantage of specialty selling is that not every manufacturer will allow you to sell its items on eBay. You may be excited about a great product only to discover that you must have a physical retail storefront in order to purchase the products for resale.

Do not be discouraged by these disadvantages. You can still make an excellent profit and build a solid eBay business by specialty selling. What I recommend, however, as the best way to specialty sell is in a "niche market."

Mass Market vs. Niche Market

Mass market refers to items that have appeal to the masses. A niche market is a much smaller segment of a larger market. It has much smaller appeal to the masses but still has high demand and, best of all, less competition.

Generally speaking, selling mass-market items is where the activity is on eBay. Selling niche market items, however, is where the profit is. To build a solid business on eBay, you need and want profit. Therefore, if you are going to specialty sell, you need a niche.

Take a simple test. Ask several of your co-workers how many of them have a cell phone. Probably all their hands will go up. Cell phones are a mass-market product that can be purchased easily and everywhere. Now ask how many of them are interested in candle making. You might find 1 hand out of 50 that would be raised. Candle making is not only a hobby, it's a specialty niche market.

You can sell mass-market items, but you need to be aware that the competition is huge, and the profit margins can be small. This is especially true on eBay. I have found from experience that the way to compete in mass-market items is as follows:

- Don't sell the new units, sell the accessories to the new units, or …

- Purchase liquidation or refurbished products from reputable sources and therefore sell older model units, or …

- Both

Therefore, if you want to sell mass-market items, you will most likely general sell them, not niche sell. When I purchased my last cell phone in the mall, I asked the salesman for the charger cord to use in my car's cigarette lighter. He told me they don't carry those types of cords. I asked him where I could get one and he said, "I recommend eBay. Are you familiar with eBay, Mr. Boyd?" Of course, eBay!

What do you think your chance is of making any profit at all selling new cell phones on eBay? No chance. Most are given away free or at a substantial discount when you enroll in a one- or two-year agreement. However, all the add-ons that people want for their cell phones, such as chargers, belt holders, and decorative face plates, are a perfect example of selling accessories for mass-market items. These are items you can get directly from manufacturers, distributors, or liquidators.

For many years, I sold marine electronics on eBay. The profit margins on new units for these items are slim on eBay. Nevertheless, I made a nice profit selling discontinued models that I obtained from liquidation sites and made even more money selling all the required accessories. That was my niche market.

Think about it for a moment. Why sell new, mass-market units that any customer can get at his or her local audio, video, phone, or sporting goods store without paying for shipping? Your competition is enormous.

I knew a Gold PowerSeller (his sales averaged between $10,000 and $25,000 a month) selling consumer electronics on eBay. However, he told me he wasn't making any profit and asked me for a consultation. He was moving a lot of product, but he was barely making enough to cover what he had spent to purchase the products. When I examined what he was doing, the problem was immediately obvious. He was trying to sell new consumer electronic products that customers could buy at their local retail store.

We determined, however, that once the customers got the products home, they would soon realize they needed accessories like extension cables, mounting brackets, stands, cases, and special cables that connect to their PCs, speakers, or other peripheral devices. Those audio, video, phone, and sporting goods stores don't usually carry all of those items that were specific for his units. Guess where the customer goes to find them? The Internet and eBay! We switched him from selling the main units to the accessories, and his business became profitable.

An Ideal Niche Market

An "ideal niche market" is a term I coined and is usually where I try to sell. It is a niche market that has high demand but very low competition. Finding an ideal niche market requires more effort than just a niche market. However, the benefits are well worth the effort, as ideal niches are very profitable. In effect, you can corner the eBay market for these products.

Using our previous example, selling the cell phone would be mass market. Selling cell phone accessories such as cases and chargers would be a niche market. Selling devices that can only be used on certain models of phones (very-hard-to-find items) is a potential ideal niche market. I say "potential" because it does not qualify until you have verified that there is high demand and low competition. If it indeed is an ideal market, you will be pleasantly surprised how the profits build.

The obvious question then is, "So how can I determine the demand and competition?" By conducting market research on eBay.

For now, the more appropriate question is, "Will you general sell or niche sell?" Answer this question first to help guide you to the right product choices when you are generating product ideas.

3 The Product Analysis Methodology

You no doubt have heard the phrase "the early bird gets the worm." In business terms, this means that early birds are market leaders. They are the biggest kids on the block in terms of sales volume. They usually are also on the cutting edge of their market, developing or selling the very latest products.

Along with the status of market leader also comes the biggest risks. Market leaders enter uncharted territory with new, unproven products. They are rewarded when they are right, but many times they are wrong.

There are market leaders on eBay as well. They may list several hundred products at any given time. They look very intimidating to the average eBay seller who wants to compete in the same market.

There is another saying that I like better than the one about the early bird. It is that "the second mouse gets the cheese." Because the trap sprung on the first mouse, the second one can easily come along and eat the cheese. The second mouse may not be the first to find the biggest hunk of cheese, but it has the lowest risk.

In business terms, the second mouse is called a market follower. This means that he doesn't lead the pack and assume the risk. He follows the pack, avoids the risks, makes fewer product investment mistakes, and sells only products that are proven to be profitable. That is exactly how I run my eBay business and how I have developed my product analysis methodology.

Overview of the Product Analysis Methodology

The methodology detailed in this book is a market follower strategy. Using this methodology, you are going to be the second mouse.

On eBay, you will play it safe. Your primary goal is not to have the most listings or the most sales but that all your products are profitable.

You will not take the first nibble. Instead, you will purposely let your market-leading competitors list all sorts of products. You simply wait for them to spring the trap, and then you will walk in and get the cheese.

This will be accomplished by finding what is hot on eBay and then conducting further analysis to ensure that the hot products are also profitable. Only then do you purchase those items to sell on eBay.

Listed here, in summary form, is the product analysis methodology we will be using throughout this book:

Step 1. Conduct Product Idea Research

- Determine whether to "general sell" or "specialty sell"
- Record product ideas
- Find the hot items
- Spy on your competition to find its best-selling products

Step 2. Conduct Product Profitability Research

- Analyze price, cost, demand, and competition
- Perform financial analysis to ensure profitability
- Determine your products

Step 3. Find Reputable Product Suppliers

- Find reputable suppliers
- Order your products

Step 4. Create Professional Listings

- Spy on top sellers to see how they list their products
- Incorporate advanced listing strategies

Step 5. Grow Your Business

- Open your eBay Store
- Sell internationally
- Manage your inventory
- Provide superior customer service
- Get your business license
- Open new niches with new products

Product Development Notebook

I designed the Product Development Notebook early in my eBay selling experience because I needed to organize my product idea research. I was writing product ideas on yellow sticky notes, napkins, newspapers, and notepads. Product ideas and plans didn't always occur to me at convenient times. I soon had scraps of paper and lots of ideas but no place or way to compile my thoughts.

Your ideas and methodology will be organized in your Product Development Notebook. This three-ring binder will become invaluable to you because it will contain your product sourcing research and analysis worksheets. You will refer to the notebook so often that you will want to keep it nearby.

SEE ALSO **Appendix C, "Product Development Notebook"**

You begin the methodology (Step 1) by recording your product ideas on the #1. Product Idea Worksheet. The remainder of the notebook will then take your initial ideas and guide you through more detailed analysis. As you go through the process of product elimination, most will be purged. Fortunately, you will be left with a few gold nuggets.

Your Product Development Notebook is your "prospecting pan." Use it to organize and record your analysis, sift through the products, and find your gold nuggets. These will be the products that you will sell on eBay.

#1. Product Idea Worksheet (Manual)

List all product ideas below. Use additional lines if necessary.

Product Idea Keywords Category	Manufacturer Contact Information (*name, phone, website, e-mail, blog*)	Competition Total # Listed on eBay	Total Sold (*Green Prices*)	Sell-Through Percent (*Sold ÷ Listed*)	Average Selling Price (*ASP*)	Passed All Tests ✓

#1. Product Idea Worksheet (Manual)

Get a Mini Notepad

I suggest that you keep a pocket-size, mini notepad with you or close by at all times. Guys, keep one in your front pocket along with a pen. Ladies, keep one in your purse. When you see or hear about a potential product, record it in your notepad. Later, when you conduct your product analysis, you will transfer these ideas to the Product Idea Worksheets.

Download the Worksheets

This book will guide you through the detailed steps for completing each worksheet. There are examples of the worksheets throughout the book and also in Appendix C.

You will need to download the blank worksheets for use in your own binder. Go to www.trainingu4auctions.com/notebook and download the worksheets (free of charge). Note that these are PDF files, so you will need a PDF reader such as Adobe Acrobat in order to read and print them. If you do not have Adobe or a PDF reader, follow the instructions provided to download and install Adobe. The worksheets and the Adobe PDF reader are free.

Once you have downloaded a copy of each worksheet, print them and take them to a copy center to save on the cost of reproduction. You are permitted to make as many copies of the worksheets as you require. In fact, that statement is actually printed on each worksheet, so you will have no copyright violation problems at the copy center.

The notebook will fill up fast. You will need to make several copies of each worksheet on three-hole paper. The worksheets will display landscape (wide) rather than portrait (long). Therefore, make sure the holes are always at the top of the sheets when viewing them landscape.

Purchase a minimum of two 1-inch, three-ring binders that have a clear plastic sleeve on the front cover. Complete a Product Development Notebook Coversheet for each binder and place it in the plastic sleeve. You should now have enough worksheets and notebooks to begin your analysis.

Product Development Notebook

Book # _____

Name: _____

If found, please call (_____) _____

Product Development Notebook Coversheet

Recommended Software Analysis Tools

In the next few chapters, you will learn the specific steps of the product analysis methodology. You should know that the process will require significant market research on eBay. In fact, one of the first steps is to determine if your product has a favorable combination of sales, demand, and competition both on the Internet and on eBay. To perform this analysis yourself usually would be tedious and take an enormous amount of time, as you would be analyzing hundreds or even thousands of listings. The good news is that you can perform this step with the analysis tools of HammerTap and Worldwide Brands's Instant Market Research (IMR) in about 20 seconds each.

You can complete the remainder of the methodology without these tools, but you will be missing the most important ingredients for product decision making. The difference in your invested time, effort, and the accuracy of your analysis when using these two tools compared to not using them is certainly considerable. In my eBay classes, I want my students to be aware of as many options as possible so that they can choose what is best for their level of selling. The key is that you know what is available and then adapt the information for your particular challenges and goals.

I am going to assume that you are serious about your eBay selling because you are reading this book. My suggestion is to get the right tools for the job. Many successful eBay PowerSellers that I know use both HammerTap and Instant Market Research to find and analyze their products. Let's take a quick look at both tools.

HammerTap requires a monthly subscription, and Worldwide Brands's IMR has a one-time fee for a lifetime membership. Both tools are very reasonably priced. If eBay is going to be your business, you should start benefiting from them right away. Remember also that the fees for these tools are tax deductible for your eBay business.

HammerTap

While there are other eBay research tools on the market, I use and recommend HammerTap. It is designed specifically to perform in-depth eBay product research and analysis very quickly.

Results		Listing Success Rate (LSR)
Total Listings	140	57.14 %
Listings with Sale	80	
Listing Success Rate (LSR)	57.14%	
Average Sales Price (ASP)	$21.18	
Total Sales	$2,456.60	
Sellers with Sale	49	42.86 %
Average Sales Per Seller	2.37	▣ Listings With Sale
Average Revenue Per Seller	$50.13	▣ Listings W/Out Sale

What do I want answered?
What Category should I list my product in?
Which day should I end my listing?
Which enhancements should I use?
Should I sell my product on eBay?
What title keywords should I use?

HammerTap Research Results

With HammerTap, you can scour the eBay marketplace and get details about specific products and how well they have been performing on eBay. This information eliminates the guesswork and leads to successful listings and profitable products. In particular, you will be using HammerTap to perform the following analyses:

SEE ALSO **Appendix B, "How to Use HammerTap"**

Market Analysis

- Determine if a category is worth pursuing.

- Find a profitable niche within the category.

- Competition—analyze the top sellers.

- Discover the top sellers' most successful products.

Product Analysis

- Find the top-performing products.

- Analyze historical data for seasonal items.

- Supply—discover the number of listings.

- Demand—analyze the successful listings.

- Sales—determine the average selling price of a certain product.

- Demand/sales ratio—discover the chances of profitability when selling a certain product.

- Analyze the top sellers of a certain product to discover how they create their listing. You will then mimic their methods and expect the same or better results.

HammerTap is usually chosen by advanced eBay sellers over the other research tools because of the level of detail and flexibility of this desktop application. Best of all, while the analysis is complex, it is very easy to use and simple to understand. HammerTap also outshines its competitors in user training.

You can receive a 10-day free trial plus a special discount rate at www.hammertap.com/studentrate.

Worldwide Brands's Product Sourcing Membership

Worldwide Brands's (WWB) Product Sourcing Membership provides access to databases of hundreds of reputable light-bulk, standard, and large-volume wholesalers, importers, liquidators, and drop shippers. Therefore, once you have discovered which products to sell, you will use WWB's databases to find reputable suppliers.

WWB's membership also provides access to the most valuable tools you can use for conducting Internet product marketing analysis. Their Instant Market Research (IMR) tools allow you to discover what the hot products, categories, and niches are on the Internet. This is an important step in your methodology because many buyers on eBay actually started their product search on the Internet.

SEE ALSO **Appendix A, "How to Use Instant Market Research"**

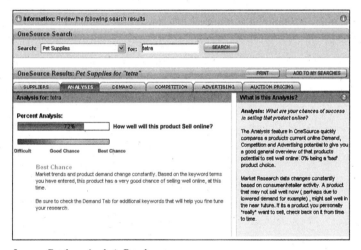

Instant Product Analysis Results

Using IMR, you simply enter the keyword of the product or category that you are interested in selling. The tool will then provide six reports for that category, niche, or product with the following information:

- Demand research
- Competition research
- Advertising research

- Pricing research
- Instant product analysis
- Suppliers of the product

Until recently, all of Worldwide Brands's databases and analysis tools were sold separately. It now offers all of its products, including the Instant Market Research tools, in one bundled offering called Product Sourcing Membership for a one-time payment and lifetime membership. They also offer excellent, optional training called The Whole$ale eBiz Education program. You can purchase the Product Sourcing Membership package separately or combined with their eBiz Education at a special discount at www.worldwidebrands.com/studentrate.

Both HammerTap and Worldwide Brands's Instant Market Research tools provide useful information that can easily be adapted to whatever selling level you are. With these two tools, you will have all the information you need for the product analysis methodology you will use for this book.

Product Idea Research

Do you already know what products you want to sell? Before you answer "yes," are you sure? Don't answer "yes" simply because you have an idea what you want to sell. Have you actually done detailed, formal research on eBay to determine that the products you are about to sell will be profitable? If the answer is still "yes," kudos to you. You have hit a home run your first time at the plate. You are an exception, though, because this is rare.

Most new sellers have no idea what to sell, and others choose the wrong products. I have spoken to many new eBay sellers who were convinced they knew what they were going to sell. However, when I would speak with them again six months later, they had already stopped selling those items and moved on to products that were more profitable. They had guessed wrong. The operative word here is "guessed."

I know of one student who started out selling baby clothes. After limited success, she attended one of my classes and learned the methodology that is now in this book. She found new products in a new niche and now successfully sells auto accessories.

No matter how confident you are about the products you will begin with, at some point you will need to research new products. Therefore, you will begin the first step of your product analysis methodology by learning how to conduct product idea research.

Generate Excellent Product Ideas

After reading Chapter 2, you know what products you should avoid selling. Now the fun begins—generating product ideas. If you are on the go, you will write these ideas in your notepad. If you are at home, use the #1. Product Idea Worksheet in your notebook.

#1. Product Idea Worksheet (Manual)

List all product ideas below. Use additional lines if necessary.

Product Idea Keywords Category	Manufacturer Contact Information (name, phone, website, e-mail, blog)	Competition Total # Listed on eBay	Total Sold (Green Prices)	Sell-Through Percent (Sold ÷ Listed)	Average Selling Price (ASP)	Passed All Tests ✔
Sony DVD Player FX820	www.sony.com					
B&D Hedge Hog Trimmer 24"	www.blackanddecker.com					
B&D Leaf Blower BV2500	www.blackanddecker.com					
Weed Grip Gel Work Gloves	www.glovesrus.com					
HP Photosmart Printer C4180	www.hp.com					

#1. Product Idea Worksheet (Manual)

Note that there are two versions of the #1. Product Idea Worksheet. Use the Manual version if you do not have the HammerTap or Instant Market Research analysis tools. Manual just means that you will be determining the numbers yourself. If you have the analysis tools, then use the #1. Worksheet for Analysis Tools to record your ideas.

As you read across the columns of the sample #1. Product Idea Worksheet, you can see the type of information you will need to gather in order to complete the form. In this product idea–generating phase, however, we are only interested in initial information such as the name of the item, the category, and especially the relevant keywords. Also record any manufacturer information for the product that you find. This information will help you conduct further analysis later.

Ideas will come to you at any time: some during a formal review process, most when you are out, and others at inconvenient times (in the shower or at 2 A.M.). Keep your notebook or notepad handy and don't be too concerned about all the remaining details in the worksheet. For now, just record your product ideas.

Start with What You Know

When thinking of product ideas, you should begin with what you know. What hobbies or areas of interest do you have? Are you an expert or very knowledgeable about a certain skill, item, or craft?

For example, say you have an interest in potpourri, scented soaps, and candles. Okay, can you narrow the hobby to just specialty candles? Good, now let's narrow it even further. What if you sold a few specialty candles plus the tools, books, wax, molds, scents, and other products that your customers can use to make their own candles? Write down whatever products pop out at you as a "YES!" during this type of brainstorming.

Turn on Your eBay Radar

A second way to find product ideas is to search off of eBay to discover unique products. To accomplish this, you need to learn how to turn on your eBay radar. This means that, as an eBay seller, you need always to be looking for products that may be a success on eBay.

Do family members, friends, or co-workers talk about an item that is difficult to find in stores or on the Internet? Listen to them carefully; you just may have discovered an idea worth pursuing.

Peter Lynch was one of the most successful mutual fund managers ever. He managed the Fidelity Fund. One of his methods for finding new companies to invest in was to take his teenage daughters to the mall and follow them around. They would always search out the latest, trendiest stores and products. He would then investigate those companies and products as a potential investment. What a simple, nontechnical approach. Yet it worked!

When you shop at the stores that you visit most often, it is quite likely you go down the same aisles picking up the same products. Next time you shop, stroll down other aisles and departments. Scan everything on the shelves looking for products that you did not know even existed or had ever thought about selling.

You are not necessarily looking for any certain product; you are generating ideas. At this stage of the process, it is not always products that are of interest but ideas for products.

Look for ideas in the yellow pages, when scanning magazines, and especially in the Sunday paper. Don't skip over the ads, study them. Note any products or ideas that pop out at you as a "YES!"

Conduct Formal Product Research

There is a product idea ritual that I do once a quarter, and I suggest you make this part of your routine as well. I take my Product Development Notebook to a local bookstore that has a huge magazine selection. I look for magazines on hobbies or topics I have never been interested in before. I then sit in a quiet area and flip through the magazines looking for the "YES!" products and idea inspiration.

When you do this, products and ideas will start jumping out at you. Again, it is not always the actual products you see that will interest you, but one product may generate a great idea for another product. For example, reviewing an ad for swimming pool filter pumps may give you an idea to sell chemistry test kits for pools.

Many times the manufacturer will be listed as well as its website. Sometimes you will see ads with the words "dealer inquiries welcome." That could mean that it may be a small manufacturer, and you can purchase the item directly from the manufacturer and not a wholesaler. Lower costs mean higher profits. Perfect! Write it all down.

Look for consumable products. There is no better product model than selling popular consumables. The swimming pool chemistry test kit is a good example. Your customers will be back every few months to purchase more testing supplies.

Look at the back pages of magazines and make a list of websites, clubs, and blogs that are relevant to this magazine. This is especially important if the magazine involves a hobby. Add your latest information to the idea worksheet columns so you can refer to it when you proceed with your analysis. The column "Product Type" will help you group all related items together later when you conduct in-depth analysis.

Okay, now you have some homework to do. Go online to all those blogs and websites. What products have you discovered on these websites? Is anything jumping out at you? Write it down.

Do you know the main reason why people use the Internet? To solve a problem. It could be health problems, not being able to locate a product, wanting to lose weight, to stop their dog from running away, and so on. They go to the Internet and use keywords to search for the solution to their problem. Many times, after conducting an Internet search, they will see the link on the results page that says, "Find this item on eBay!" Here they come looking for the solution to their problem on eBay. Someone needs to solve it for them, why not you?

Therefore, find a problem and then find and sell the product that solves the problem. Go to the hobbyist websites and view their products. Do they solve a problem? What are the hobbyists saying on the blogs? Are they complaining about a problem? Pull up that blog posting and read the responses. Many times someone will respond with a solution by touting a great new product they have discovered. Do they mention who manufactures it? Write it all down.

Find What's Hot on eBay

Another place to generate product ideas is the "What's Hot" link on eBay. Available for your review from eBay's Seller Central is the "What's Hot" product predictions for different categories. Here's how to find it:

1. Select **Site Map** at the top of any page, and select **What's Hot** from the link list under **Selling Resources**.

2. Now scroll down the major categories and click on the link for a category that you are interested in selling.

Scan the lists looking for categories and items that attract you and are worth further investigation. These are all products that the eBay merchandising team predicts to be hot sellers based on marketing research from industry experts. We will still need to use the profitability worksheet later to make sure they are profitable. For now, though, we are brainstorming for potential products, and instead of sifting through millions of products on eBay, we are looking at only the items predicted by eBay's merchandising team to be hot. Record any good prospects on your Product Idea Worksheet.

Identify New Trends

This method of identifying new trends for our product ideas is a slight departure from our methodology because, rather than using research on past data, we are predicting trends. While this method seems contrary, it can be very worthwhile. Market leaders, when they choose correctly, can make a lot of money.

Every product has a life cycle. Successful products have an introduction, growth, maturity, and declining cycle phase. Most eBay sellers sell items on the declining side of the product life cycle. They sell items from liquidators, older models, refurbished products, and used items. They are squeezing the last bit of juice out of the orange before it is thrown out.

When you include trending as part of your methodology, you are in the growth phase or the incline of the product life cycle. You are ahead of the crowd, in fact leading the crowd, and are hence a market leader. The best part is that when you find your niche products in a new trend, you can ride the wave of sales for a considerable period of time.

SEE ALSO **Chapter 12, "The eBay Product Life Cycle"**

How do you identify the new, hot trends and their associated products? Research. You especially need to stay current in the categories in which you sell. Subscribe to related magazines, newsletters, and websites. Attend related trade shows.

Researching outside of the categories you are familiar with, however, is where you will most likely find the biggest moneymakers and newest trends. Trying to find these discoveries on your own can be a time-consuming and daunting task. Let's get professional help.

Would you like some excellent trend analysis information specific to the eBay marketplace? I will tell you my best source for eBay product trending secrets: What Do I Sell® (WDIS).

The founder and CEO of What Do I Sell®, Lisa Suttora, is an expert in eBay product sourcing. She is a certified eBay information and service provider and a contributing editor to *Entrepreneur* magazine and the Product Sourcing Radio show. She has been invited to be a featured speaker every year since 2005 at eBay Live (eBay's huge international annual convention).

She maintains a members-only website for sellers who want to get the edge on their competition and find reputable sources of products to sell. I use her site faithfully as part of my methodology when searching liquidator sites. She has a remarkable record of accomplishment for discovering the latest trends and the next hot products on eBay.

Her site is also full of product sourcing information, tutorials, practical strategies, and tips on how to generate ideas for new products. I believe a membership to her site is essential for any serious seller moving from Phase I to Phase II in the eBay selling progression. Most importantly, her site is ideal for the product idea phase of your methodology. You will be pleasantly surprised and inspired when you see how comprehensive her website is. Her rates are also significantly discounted when using this student rate link www.whatdoisell.com/ studentrate. Note that you will see the special discount after you choose her Business Premium package during checkout (scroll down the checkout page to see her generous discount).

Spy on Your Giant Competitors

This method of product idea research should be used if you are already an eBay seller and need to add new items to your product line. It can also be used when you are considering items in a particular category but have no experience selling in that category. In both cases, you are going to do some James Bond spy work on your biggest competitors.

Do you sell in categories (or want to) that have a lot of competition? Are some of them large competitors that list hundreds of items? I would bet you are a bit intimidated by them. I certainly was when I first started selling on eBay. Then I thought, instead of being intimidated, why not snoop through their listings and look for product ideas? I found that this actually worked. I further refined my methods to become a "super spy" of eBay investigative techniques.

Later in this book, I detail how to conduct research on eBay by looking at only the completed listings to determine what sold, what price it sold for, or at what price(s) it didn't sell. Did you know you can do the same thing for individual sellers—namely, your largest competitors?

SEE ALSO **Chapter 7, "eBay Research"**

By using the following method, you can easily discover specific products your competitors are selling, what price they are receiving, and avoid the vast majority of their products that are not selling. Then you will carry only the items that are proven to sell and are profitable! In effect, you are spying on a giant competitor in order to "cherry pick" only its best-selling products.

Go ahead and let your big competitors list 300 to 800 products. Don't be intimidated at all. View them as merely the "market testers" for your new product ideas. You spy on them, discover what items are hot sellers, and then add them to your product idea list. Wow, what a concept! Did I just relieve a lot of competition intimidation? It gets even better. Next I will explain the specific steps you should use to become a super spy.

Giant Competitor Spy Sheet

Here are the specific steps to spy on your giant competitors. You will find and then cherry pick your competitor's best-selling products. The worksheet we will use for this step is #2. Giant Competitor Spy Worksheet. Complete a worksheet for each major competitor. Note that there are two versions of this worksheet. Use the Manual version if you do not have analysis tools. Use the Analysis Tools version if you have HammerTap and Instant Market Research.

If you know which product you want to sell, then first you need to find the top sellers of those products:

1. From eBay's homepage, select the **Advanced Search** link on the quick search bar.

2. Scroll down the left-hand side of the page and click on **Find Stores.**

3. In the **Enter keyword or Store name** field, type the keyword of the product you are interested in selling. Select the button **Stores with matching items** and click the **Search** button.

   You will now see a list of all eBay Stores that sell that product. The stores will be listed in order based on the number of matching items. If it is a small list or they have few products in their stores, you are at too deep a level. Back up a level by determining what category the product is in, and then perform an advanced search in that category (using the category drop-down menu). You are looking for your biggest competitors that have a lot of products listed in the category you are interested in selling.

4. Now click on the first giant's eBay Store. You will see a list of products. Click on any product.

5. Under the **Meet the Seller** field, next to **View seller's other items,** select **List.** You are now viewing all items that are currently for sale by this seller. You now need to see how the sales have performed in the last two weeks.

6. Scroll down the left-hand column and select the **Completed listings** checkbox. Then click the **Show Items** button near the bottom. You are now viewing all the items that have

completed (the listing has ended) for this particular seller in the last two weeks.

7. In the **Sort by** drop-down menu, choose **Price: highest first.** You are now viewing the top-selling items for this seller in the last two weeks.

When you do this you will be amazed. Observe what products have sold (prices in green) and those that did not sell (prices in red). Many times you will see listing after listing that has ended in red as a no sale. Even more, the particular product that attracted you in the first place may be continually showing up in red as a no sale!

What? No sale? You mean that all these products that this top competitor is listing are going unsold? A resounding "YES" and you have the proof! This seller is losing money. He is not attracting any buyers to these listings. This seller doesn't look quite so giant-sized or intimidating anymore. But we are just getting started, and now the real fun begins.

Continue to scan this seller's listings from top to bottom looking specifically for the green price, meaning the item ended in a sale. If you see any product that has potential, record the competitor, product keywords, and the competitor's average selling price (approximate) in the specific columns provided on the #2 worksheet.

You will find new products that you never thought would be a good seller on eBay. But there they are in green, jumping out at you from your competitor's sales history. What I also find interesting about this process is that some items that I originally thought would be top sellers aren't selling at all. Then other items I thought were dull, uninteresting, or I never even considered are selling like hotcakes.

Continue this process until you have exhausted this competitor's sales history. You will probably have a list of about 10 to 50 products that consistently sell.

Continue this process and complete a new, separate #2. Giant Competitor Spy Worksheet for every giant competitor selling the types of products you are interested in. Now compare your worksheets. If you see the same product being successfully sold (green price) by other sellers, place a check mark in the column **Multiple Seller Check.**

#2. Giant Competitor Spy Worksheet (Manual)

List all product ideas below. Use additional lines if necessary.

Giant Competitor User ID: _____

Product Idea and Keywords	Category and Subcategories	Competition Total # Listed on eBay	Total Sold (Green Prices)	Sell-Through Percent (Sold ÷ Listed)	Average Selling Price (ASP)	Multiple Seller Check	Passed Initial Tests ✓
Sony DVD Player FX820		26	24	92%	$125	✓	✓
B&D Hedge Hog Trimmer 24"		63	39	62%	$64	✓	✓
B&D Leaf Blower BV2500		86	62	72%	$56	✓	✓
Weed Grip Gel Work Gloves		Not on eBay					
HP Photosmart Printer C4180		296	234	79%	$74	✓	✓

#2. Giant Competitor Spy Worksheet (Manual)

Use HammerTap to Find Your Giants

Appendix B includes instructions for how to quickly find and then spy on your eBay competitors using HammerTap. With this tool, you can quickly find your major competitors, discover their most successfully selling products (including their average selling price), and their total quantity sold for the last 30 days.

Pick a Category, Any Category

You can also use these spying techniques to scan any category on eBay for profitable products. Remember that there are over 50,000 categories and subcategories on eBay. Another method for generating product ideas then is simply to start scanning categories of interest on eBay. When you spot a category or product that you believe could be a winner, perform the steps below and record your findings on the #2. Giant Competitor Spy Sheet.

If you don't know what product you want to sell but want to check out certain categories, use the following steps:

1. If you know what category to search, select the **Advanced Search** link from the quick search bar on eBay's homepage.

2. In the **In this category** drop-down list, select your major category and click **Search.**

3. From the left-hand side, select the subcategory that interests you. Continue this process until you are at the subcategory level you desire. Many times there will be a very large number of products. Many of these items are not relevant to what you are interested in selling. If this is the case, you need to narrow the search.

4. To narrow a category search, you need to eliminate irrelevant products. Use the **Back** button to get back to the category search screen of Advanced Search. Place your cursor in the **Keyword** search box and add keywords in order to narrow your search. In addition, type any keywords for items you wish to eliminate from the results in the **Exclude these words** field. Continue this process until you have a more manageable list to investigate.

5. Scroll down the left-hand column and select the **Completed listings** checkbox. Then click the **Show Items** button near the bottom. You are now viewing all the items that have completed (the listing has ended) in this category for the last two weeks.

6. In the **Sort by** drop-down menu, choose **Price: highest first.** You are now viewing the top-selling items for this category (or subcategory) in the last two weeks.

SEE ALSO **Appendix B, "Spy on Your Giant Competitors"**

But I Really, Really Want to Sell This!

Finally, this is the time to revisit your favorite products that were showing up as red (no sale). I know you are disappointed and you really want to sell that item. If your intuition has convinced you that those items still would be good sellers, consider the following possibilities to help make your decision.

- **It is a seasonal item**—The results from the red, unsold prices performed during our giant spying could be a result of the season. The product may in fact be a hot seller, but it is showing up red right now because you are viewing it off-season. Note that if you have HammerTap, you can look back up to one year in order to check on prices for a particular season.

- **Your giant competitor is a lousy eBay seller**—Maybe the product is showing up as unsold red simply because your giant competitor doesn't know how to sell the item on eBay. Before you give up on that favorite product that is showing up with red prices, leave your giant's listings for a moment and conduct a Product Search.

SEE ALSO **Chapter 5, "#1. Product Idea Worksheet (Manual)"**

Ongoing Product Ideas

Throughout this chapter, you have learned and used a number of methods to generate product ideas. All of these ideas have been recorded on either your #1. Product Idea Worksheets or #2. Giant Competitor Spy Worksheets.

I realize that this may appear to be an exhaustive research process when you are a new seller with no products. It will not be as time-consuming to add to an existing product line as it is when you are starting with no products. You will continue to use this same process throughout your eBay selling career because you will always be looking for new products and weeding out the poor performers.

Step 1 of your methodology is now complete. As you become more experienced with product idea research, you will discover that you have developed an eye for and an ability to select winners.

Prospecting for Gold Nuggets

You now have a list of solid product ideas from a variety of sources. All potential products have been recorded on either the #1. Product Idea Worksheets or #2. Giant Competitor Spy Worksheets. It doesn't really matter at this point how you have found your products, what categories they are in, or that they may be unrelated. What does matter is that you have a number of excellent prospects using the methods and sources described in Chapter 4.

In this chapter, you will learn how to perform your profitability analysis. This process may look like homework at first glance because of some basic math that will be required, but this is the last and most important step in your product analysis methodology. Learning these details before you fill a spare room, garage, or warehouse with items you can't sell is worth the time and effort expended. Mastering this methodology will make you an expert regarding your particular products in the eBay marketplace.

At the end of this process, many of your products will be eliminated, including some items that you really wanted to sell. Don't be discouraged if this happens. Eliminating high-risk products is the whole point of your methodology. On the contrary, be encouraged that you have just saved hundreds or thousands of dollars on products that would have been losers on eBay. Best of all, you will be left with products that are winners—your gold nuggets!

Completing the #1. Product Idea Worksheet

When you were writing your product ideas on your #1. worksheet, you should have written the name of the product and the relevant keywords. The manufacturer contact information should have also been added if it was known at the time. The rest of the columns remained blank. The first step in our analysis then will be to complete these worksheets.

#1. Product Idea Worksheet (Manual)

List all product ideas below. Use additional lines if necessary.

Product Idea Keywords Category	Manufacturer Contact Information (name, phone, website, e-mail, blog)	Competition Total # Listed on eBay	Total Sold (Green Prices)	Sell-Through Percent (Sold ÷ Listed)	Average Selling Price (ASP)	Passed All Tests ✓
Sony DVD Player FX820	www.sony.com	26	24	92%	$125	✓
B&D Hedge Hog Trimmer 24"	www.blackanddecker.com	63	39	62%	$64	✓
B&D Leaf Blower BV2500	www.blackanddecker.com	86	62	72%	$56	✓
Weed Grip Gel Work Gloves	www.glovesrus.com	Not on eBay				
HP Photosmart Printer C4180	www.hp.com	296	234	79%	$74	✓

#1. Product Idea Worksheet (Manual)

As a reminder, there are two versions of the #1. worksheet. If you have the HammerTap and Instant Market Research tools, then you will refer to the sections in this chapter for the #1. Product Idea Worksheet (Analysis Tools). If you do not have those tools, then refer to the sections for the #1. Product Idea Worksheet (Manual), which is next.

#1. Product Idea Worksheet (Manual)

Refer to your #1. Product Idea Worksheets (Manual). Manual simply means the information will be obtained manually (instead of with the analysis tools). We will now complete the worksheet.

Step 1. Conduct a Product Search

Column three (starting from the left) requires that you find the total number of each of your products that were listed on eBay in the last two weeks. We will use a product search methodology to find this information.

1. From eBay's homepage, select the **Advanced Search** link on the quick search bar.

2. In the **Enter Keyword or Item Number** search box, type the primary keywords that you have recorded on your #1. worksheet and click **Search.**

3. You will now see a list of all items currently for sale on eBay that include those keywords in their title.

4. Narrow the list down to the specific item by adding more keywords or eliminate certain keywords by writing them in the **Exclude these words field** (from the Advanced Search page).

5. Once you have removed the outliers by narrowing the search to your specific product, you will see all the items currently for sale on eBay that match those keywords.

6. Now scroll down the left side under Search Options and Show Only. Click the checkbox **Completed Listings** and then click **Show Items.**

7. Now you will see all the items that match the keywords for your item that have completed (ended) on eBay during the last two weeks. The prices in green mean those items sold for that price. The prices in red mean those items did not sell.

8. Toward the top right of the screen, click on the **Sort by** drop-down box and select **Price: Highest First.**

You now are reviewing all of the listings for your item that have received the highest bids in the last two weeks. All listings that have the highest green prices (meaning they sold) are the best performers and are the ones on which you will conduct further analysis in Step 2.

Step 2. Analyze Your Product's Performance

It is very important that you narrowed your products down and removed all outliers in order to provide accurate statistics for the next steps. Also, watch for selling prices that are very low. Some sellers try to make their profit off shipping. It is too difficult to factor these sellers into our formula, so I suggest you consider them outliers and eliminate them from your data.

1. Record the total number of listings for that particular product. It is located at the top of the search results labeled **items found for.** Enter the number on your worksheet in the column **Competition Total # Listed on eBay.**

record total listings

Record Total Listings

2. Count the number of listings that ended with a green price, meaning that the product sold. You may need to page through several pages for popular items. Remember, this is the manual

process so remain patient. Enter the total number of listings that actually sold (green price) in the column **Total Sold.**

3. Divide the **Total Sold** column by the **Total # Listed** column. This will give you a decimal number. Multiply the decimal by 100 and write this percentage in the column **Sell-Through Percent.**

You now know the sell-through rate for this item on eBay for the last two weeks. This is your first test. You want your minimum percentage sell-through to equal or exceed about 60 percent. If the percentage score is below 60 percent, then the product has failed the test. You should move on to other items and not spend any further time with this product.

Note that 60 percent is not etched in stone. If you feel strongly about a product that is below 60 percent, then take it to the next step for the profitability test. However, you need to have a watermark that weeds out less desirable items, and for me, it is about 60 percent.

If the percentage score is around 60 percent or above, your item has passed the first hurdle. Place a check mark in the final column **Passed All Tests.** Now add up all of the green prices and divide that total sales number by the number in the **Total Sold** column. This is your average selling price (ASP) for that item. Record it in the **Average Selling Price** column.

Continue this process for all products on your #1. Product Idea Worksheet (Manual). When you have completed the worksheet, all products that have a check mark in the Passed All Tests column will move on to the #3. Product Profitability Worksheet.

#1. Product Idea Worksheet (Analysis Tools)

Use the process described in this section if you have the HammerTap and the Instant Market Research analysis tools. These tools are like bookends because one provides in-depth marketing analysis for the Internet and the other for eBay. Ideally, you need both tools in order to provide a complete online marketplace analysis.

To complete this section, you will use some of the steps detailed in Appendixes A and B. You will record your findings in the #1. Product Idea Worksheet (Analysis Tools).

#1. Product Idea Worksheet (Analysis Tools)

List all product ideas below. Use additional lines if necessary.

Product Idea Keywords Category	Manufacturer Contact Information (name, phone, website, e-mail, blog)	H. Tap ASP (End Day)	H. Tap LSR%	IMR Market Bar %, □ Ideal Niche	IMR Passed Demand Test ✓	IMR Passed Comp. Test ✓ □ <20	Passed All Tests ✓
Sony DVD Player FX820	www.sony.com	$125	91%	□		□	
B&D Hedge Hog Trimmer 24"	www.blackanddecker.com	$64	64%	□		□	
B&D Leaf Blower BV2500	www.blackanddecker.com	$56	71%	□		□	
Weed Grip Gel Work Gloves	www.glovesrus.com	–	–	□		□	
HP Photosmart Printer C4180	www.hp.com	$78	73%	□		□	

Record LSR and ASP

Step 1. HammerTap—Conduct a Quick Analysis

Use the steps detailed in Appendix B to perform a Quick Analysis for your item.

Step 2. HammerTap—Analyze Your Product's Performance

Follow the analysis suggested in Step 4 of the Quick Analysis methodology (Appendix B) to determine the listing success rate (LSR) and the average selling price (ASP). Record your findings in the two H. Tap columns provided on your #1. Product Idea Worksheet (Analysis Tools). Remember that the correct ASP to use is the one HammerTap provides in the row labeled End Day.

If the LSR is below 60 percent, then the product has failed the first hurdle, and you should not perform any further analysis. Move on to the next product. If the LSR is 60 percent or above, the product has passed the first hurdle and is worthy of further analysis using Instant Market Research.

Step 3. Instant Market Research (IMR)—Conduct a Product Search

First, use the process described in Appendix A to analyze a product of interest using the Instant Market Research tool. Then perform the following steps:

1. Record the Marketplace Research Results Bar percentage on your worksheet in the column **Market Bar Percentage.**

2. If any Marketplace Results Bar is greater than 90 percent, place a check mark in the small checkbox **Ideal Niche** in the same column. You may very well have just identified an ideal niche!

SEE ALSO **Chapter 2, "An Ideal Niche Market"**

3. Now click the **Demand** tab in IMR. This report analyzes major search engine data to reveal how popular the product is online. There are no absolute criteria for this analysis. However, you want a product that is getting several searches online. After you have conducted a few of these analyses, you will begin to get a feel for good product demand. I like to sell products that are getting at least 1,000 searches. If your

product has around 1,000 searches or more, it has good online demand and has passed the Demand test. Place a check in the **Passed Demand Test** column of the worksheet. If the product did not pass the Demand test, leave the column blank.

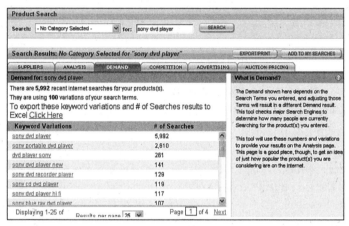

Check Demand with Instant Market Research

4. Now click the **Competition** tab. You will want relatively low competition online and on eBay in order to avoid entering a marketplace that is already saturated with sellers. You will see separate numbers for Yahoo!, Google, and eBay. Again, there is no set number that is our watermark, but the less competition you find, the better your chance for success.

A product that has several hundred competitors is of concern because your chance of competing successfully will be difficult. This number is subjective because it also depends on how popular the item is. I usually prefer to have no more than 100 eBay competitors. Ideally I would prefer less than 50, and if my competition is less than 20, I can usually be the top seller or even corner the market. You can adjust the maximum number to suit your preferences once you gain more experience. When starting to use this methodology, we will place the watermark at 100.

If your item has fewer than 100 competitors on eBay, then place a check in the **Passed Competition Test** column. If the eBay competition is less than 20, place a check in the small checkbox of the same column. This indicates very low competition and an ideal competitive market.

Product Idea Worksheet Final Analysis

You now have a comprehensive online marketplace analysis and are well equipped to make a sound product decision. Now examine the columns of the worksheet. Your product has passed this comprehensive marketplace analysis if it has the following results:

- ❏ LSR equal to or greater than 60 percent
- ❏ Market Bar equal to or greater than 60 percent
- ❏ Check mark in Passed Demand Test column
- ❏ Check mark in Passed Competition Test column

If your product has passed all of these tests, then it is worthy to move on to the #3. Product Profitability Worksheet. Place a check mark in the **Passed All Tests** column.

Any products that have check marks in either the **Ideal Niche** or **<20** mini checkboxes will be given priority placement on the Profitability worksheet. You may have just discovered a market that you can corner!

Following are some things to consider if your product fails some of the tests:

- If your product failed the LSR test from HammerTap, then forget about that product for now. You can always check it again later if marketplace conditions change.

- If the product failed the Market Bar test from IMR, it could be that you have narrowed your search too much. I have found that IMR is best used to analyze the category or niche marketplace. HammerTap is best used to analyze a specific product on eBay. If you were trying to analyze a very specific product using IMR, the results could be misleading.

  For example, using IMR, a search for the Sony DVD player model FX820 is probably too detailed. A better search would be simply Sony DVD player. IMR would then give you a good idea of the Sony DVD player online marketplace.

#1. Product Idea Worksheet (Analysis Tools)

List all product ideas below. Use additional lines if necessary.

Product Idea Keywords Category	Manufacturer Contact Information (name, phone, website, e-mail, blog)	H. Tap ASP (End Day)	H. Tap LSR%	IMR Market Bar %, □ Ideal Niche	IMR Passed Demand Test	IMR Passed Comp. Test ✓ □ <20	Passed All Tests
							✓
Sony DVD Player FX820	www.sony.com	$125	91%	□ 83%	✓	□ ✓	✓
B&D Hedge Hog Trimmer 24"	www.blackanddecker.com	$64	64%	□ 62%	✓	□ ✓	✓
B&D Leaf Blower BV2500	www.blackanddecker.com	$56	71%	□ 66%	✓	□ ✓	✓
Weed Grip Gel Work Gloves	www.glovesrus.com	–	–	□		□	
HP Photosmart Printer C4180	www.hp.com	$78	73%	□ 34%	✓	□	

#1. Product Idea Worksheet (Analysis Tools)

Therefore, if your item has a very low Market Bar percentage, back your search up a level and try it again. This is especially important if the product has already passed HammerTap's LSR test.

- If your product passed the LSR and Market Bar tests but failed the Demand and Competition tests, you have some leeway. The Demand and Competition tests are more warnings than absolutes. If, after careful thought, you still feel that a product needs further analysis, then move it on to the #3. worksheet. Just know that you should proceed with caution with this product because your methodology has just given you a warning.

Completing the Giant Competitor Spy Worksheets

If you conducted product idea research on your giant competitors or categories, then you used the #2. Giant Competitor Spy Worksheets (either Manual or Analysis Tools). You should have completed a separate #2. worksheet for each competitor and written its User ID at the top of each form so you can refer back to it later if necessary.

The columns for Keywords, Categories, and Subcategories should already have been completed. Using the process described next, you will conduct marketplace research to determine how well these products have been selling on eBay and whether they are worthy of further consideration.

#2. Giant Competitor Spy Worksheet (Manual)

The steps to complete this manual worksheet are very similar to the steps previously described for completing the #1. Product Idea Worksheet (Manual).

Step 1. Conduct a Product Search

Refer to the section in this chapter called "#1. Product Idea Worksheet (Manual)." Follow the same process described for "Step 1. Conduct a Product Search."

You will then be viewing all of the listings for your item that have received the highest bids in the last two weeks. The listings with the highest green prices are the top sellers. You will use these listings to conduct further analysis in Step 2.

Step 2. Analyze Your Product's Performance

Use the same analysis methods that were previously described in the section "Step 2. Analyze Your Product's Performance." Record the total number of listings and the total that sold (prices in green) in the columns provided. Determine the sell-through percent. Any product that does not have a sell-through rate of about 60 percent or higher has failed the test and is not worthy of further consideration. Move on to the next product.

Products that have a score of about 60 percent or above have passed the first test. Use the methods previously described in the "Step 2. Analyze Your Product's Performance" section to determine and record the average selling price.

If your product has passed the 60 percent hurdle, then it is worthy of further analysis. Place a check in the **Passed All Tests** column. Continue this process for all products on your list. The products that have passed all tests will move on to the #3. Product Profitability Worksheet.

#2. Giant Competitor Spy Worksheet (Analysis Tools)

If you have HammerTap and Instant Market Research, then you should have used the #2. worksheet version for the analysis tools. The steps to complete the remainder of the form are the same as those previously described in the "#1. Product Idea Worksheet (Analysis Tools)" section of this chapter. At the completion of the analysis, all products that have a check in the Passed All Tests column are ready to move on to the #3. Product Profitability Worksheet.

The #3. Product Profitability Worksheet

You will now determine which of the product ideas from worksheets #1. and #2. are profitable. Your first step is to take all product names that had checks in their **Passed All Tests** column and transfer them to column A of the #3. Product Profitability Worksheet. Along with the product names, also transfer the average selling price for each item to column B, **Average Selling Price.**

If you used Instant Market Research, some of your products may have had a check in the small **Ideal Niche** checkbox in the **Market Bar** column. You may also have found that you had fewer than 20 competitors on eBay in the **Passed Competition Test** column. Transfer the check marks from any of these products to the small checkboxes in column K. These will be used later to identify the products that have the absolute best chance for success if they prove profitable.

Some basic math is necessary in the next few steps. Follow the worksheet examples provided in the book as you complete your worksheets the first few times. It won't be long before you can complete this process very quickly.

Determine Your Margin and Profit Requirements

Profitability is based on both price and cost. The cost of a product may be dependent on where you obtain the item. If it is from a general item supplier such as surplus or liquidation, it can be considerably cheaper than buying specialty products from a wholesaler. In either case, you want to ensure that your products will bring enough profit to make the effort of listing, selling, and shipping them worthwhile.

Professional business managers determine this for their products and services by using a minimum profit margin percentage. Any product or service that does not meet their minimum percentage is not worth selling. You will want to perform the same thresholds for your products. Before you begin further analysis of your products, you must first determine your minimum margin and profit requirements.

Minimum Profit

To determine your minimum profit, ask yourself this question: What is the lowest profit a product should yield before it is not worth selling? The answer is up to you. For my products, I want to make a profit of at least $10.

#3. Product Profitability Worksheet

List all qualified products from Worksheet #1. or #2. Use two lines if necessary.

Your minimum Profit Margin Requirement is ___25%___ *(25% is suggested)*

Your minimum Profit Requirement is ___$10___ *($10 is suggested)*

A. Product Name	B. Avg. Selling Price (ASP)	C. Retail MSRP (Manuf. Website)	D. Est. Cost (C × 50%)	E. eBay and PayPal Fees (B × Fee%)	F. Profit B − (D + E)	G. Margin% (F ÷ B) × 100	H. Meets Min. Profit	I. Meets Min. Margin	J. Passed Product Eval. Test	K. Passed All Tests ✓
							✓	✓	✓	□ I.N. □ < 20
Sony DVD Player FX820	$125									□ I.N. □ < 20
B&D Hedge Hog Trim	$64									□ I.N. □ < 20
B&D Blower BV2500	$56									□ I.N. □ < 20

Record Minimum Profit and Margin

Most of the products I sell bring much higher profits, some into the hundreds of dollars. However, my minimum is $10. Remember also that this is $10 in profit, not a $10 selling price. Profit is determined by subtracting the cost of the product and the eBay and PayPal fees from the item's selling price. We will perform this step later in the worksheet. For now, decide what your minimum profit must be and record it in the space provided toward the top of the #3. worksheet.

Minimum Profit Margin

Many people confuse profit margin with profit markup. They are not the same. If an eBay seller says he wants to mark up his items by 100 percent, he means he wants to double his money. This is also referred to in the retail industry as a keystone price. With keystone, then, if your product costs you $20, you want to sell it for $40. Markup, however, is not margin. In fact, a 100 percent markup is actually a 50 percent margin. Business managers use margin, not markup, to analyze their products and so will we for our methodology.

Profit margin is a ratio of profit over sales price (P/SP) and is presented as a percentage. It reveals whether the profit from a product or service is appropriate for its sales price. You want all your products to be "pulling their weight," and profit margin will tell you if they are.

For example, maybe you have a $10 minimum profit requirement for all your products. One product costs you $5 and sells for $15. It meets your $10 minimum profit requirement. You have another product that costs you $1,000 and you sell it for $1,010. It also meets your minimum profit requirement. Which product is the best one for you to sell?

Obviously, the best product is the $5 product because it costs $995 less to stock than the other product, yet it produces the same profit. That is the purpose of using profit margin when analyzing your products. You want your products to produce a minimum ratio of profit to sales price, or it is not worth selling. We will perform this step a bit later in our spreadsheet completion process.

So, what is a good minimum profit margin for eBay selling? It depends on the source of your product. If you niche or specialty sell, then the source of your products will most likely be wholesalers. These suppliers offer their products to you at roughly half the retail price. Therefore, about the best you can hope to do is double your money. Remember that doubling your money is a 50 percent margin. So 50 percent is your ceiling of maximum potential.

SEE ALSO **Chapter 2, "Specialty Market Selling"**

Based on my experience in selling eBay items, I like my minimum margin to be half the percent of my maximum potential. Therefore, my minimum margin requirement is 25 percent for products I will purchase from wholesalers.

If I purchase items from liquidators, surplus, or other drastically reduced cost suppliers, my minimum margin would be higher. I like products from those suppliers to be about 60 percent margin or greater.

In either case, no matter the type of supplier, my minimum would still be 25 percent margin and $10 profit. The combination of those two components will produce a product that is still worth selling. You can use my numbers or develop your own over time. Whatever you determine, write your minimum profit margin and profit requirements at the top of the #3. worksheet before you begin further analysis.

Completing the #3. Product Profitability Worksheet

Your #3. worksheet should now contain the product name and average selling price for your products that have passed all tests thus far. You will now perform the math required to complete the worksheet. Refer to the #3. Product Profitability Worksheet when performing the math. We will use the Sony DVD player FX280 as our example. Get your calculator and then let's get started.

Determine the Retail MSRP (Column C)

If you know the cost that you will pay for your product (from liquidators, surplus stores, and so on), skip column C and enter it directly in column D. If you are unsure, then you have to assume you will be purchasing it from wholesalers so use an estimate.

#3. Product Profitability Worksheet

List all qualified products from Worksheet #1. or #2. Use two lines if necessary.

Your minimum Profit Margin Requirement is ___25%___ *(25% is suggested)*

Your minimum Profit Requirement is ___$10___ *($10 is suggested)*

A. Product Name	B. Avg. Selling Price (ASP)	C. Retail MSRP (Manuf. Website)	D. Est. Cost (C × 50%)	E. eBay and PayPal Fees (B × Fee%)	F. Profit B – (D + E)	G. Margin% (F ÷ B) × 100	H. Meets Min. Profit	I. Meets Min. Margin	J. Passed Product Eval. Test ✓	K. Passed All Tests ✓ ☐ I. Niche ☐ < 20
Sony DVD Player FX820	$125	$154	$77	$8.75	$39.25	31%	✓	✓	✓	☐ I.N. ☐ < 20
B&D Hedge Hog Trim	$64	Outlet Mall on Sale	$45	$5.12	$13.88	22%	✓			☐ I.N. ☐ < 20
B&D Blower BV2500	$56	Liquida- tor	$14	$4.48	$37.52	67%	✓	✓	✓	☐ I.N. ☐ < 20

#3. Product Profitability Worksheet (Completed)

Many manufacturers list the retail price of their items on their websites. You can conduct an Internet search for the manufacturer, or you can usually find them using www.thomasnet.com.

If you are having a difficult time finding the manufacturer, search the Internet to find other online sellers of the product. Many times they will list the retail price alongside their discounted price. If you have Instant Market Research, conduct a Product Search and then use the Advertising Tab to see the top sellers of that product online. Record the full retail price (MSRP) in column C.

Determine the Estimated Cost (Column D)

Most wholesalers offer products at 40 to 50 percent off the manufacturer's suggested retail price (MSRP). For your methodology, use 50 percent. Multiply the MSRP by 50 percent and enter the estimated cost in column D.

Formula to Estimate Your Cost (D):

Column C × .5 = Estimated Cost (D)

Sony DVD Player Example:

$154 × .5 = $77

Estimate the eBay and PayPal Fees (Column E)

Both the eBay and PayPal fees will vary depending on your starting price, your selling format (Auction-Style, Fixed Price, Store, or Best Offer), any enhancements you have added to the listing, and the final selling price. EBay also adjusts their fees frequently.

However, for our worksheet, we must make an average estimate for the combined eBay and PayPal fees based on the average selling price. The following table is provided for you to quickly estimate the average percentage for your total eBay and PayPal fees. Use the table only as a rule of thumb for this worksheet. If you prefer specific fee calculations, go to www.ebcalc.com.

Average of Total eBay and PayPal Fees per ASP	
ASP	Total Fee %
Less than $50	10%
$50–$100	8%
$100–$500	7%
$500–$1,000	6%
$1,000 or more	5%

Use the average selling price (ASP) in column B along with the preceding table to estimate your total eBay and PayPal fee percentage for your product. Multiply your ASP in column B by this percentage and enter the estimated fees in column E.

Formula to Estimate Your Fees (E):

Column B × Fee % = eBay and PayPal Fees (E)

Sony DVD Player Example:

$125 × 7% = $8.75

Estimate Your Profit (Column F)

Estimating your profit will be another two-step process. You need to add your product cost to your estimated eBay and PayPal fees and then subtract that total cost from your ASP. Enter your estimated profit in column F.

Formula to Estimate Your Profit (F):

Column B – (Columns D + E) = Profit (F)

Sony DVD Player Example:

$125 – ($77 + $8.75) = $39.25

You are on a roll! Let's continue the math and do just one more equation.

Determine Your Margin (Column G)

As discussed earlier in this chapter, profit margin is a ratio of profit divided by average selling price, and it is displayed as a percentage.

You simply divide column F by column B and multiply the decimal by 100 to determine the percentage. Enter the percentage in column G.

Formula to Estimate Your Margin (G):

$(F \div B) \times 100 = \text{Margin } \% \text{ (G)}$

Sony DVD Player Example:

$(\$39.25 \div \$125) \times 100 = 31\%$

Now that you have finished the math, I want to make a point about profit margin again. Earlier I mentioned that margin is what business owners use to determine if a product is pulling its weight. The #3. worksheet example in the "Completing the #3. Profitability Worksheet" section earlier in this chapter makes my point.

Notice that both the Sony DVD player and the Black and Decker leaf blower have a similar profit (column F). But look at column G. Why is the leaf blower a 67 percent margin and the Sony player only 31 percent? It is because of their cost. The leaf blower brings in the same profit but costs you over $63 less! The leaf blower is the better use of your inventory dollars. Now you should see that it is not always profit but profit margin that is so important.

Meets Minimum Profit and Margin Requirements (Columns H and I)

You will now compare your profit and margin estimates to your minimum requirements that you entered at the top of the worksheet.

- If the profit amount in column F meets or exceeds your profit minimum, place a check mark in column H.

- If the margin percentage in column G meets or exceeds your margin requirement, place a check mark in column I.

Isn't this fun? It is if you find products that have passed all the tests to this point.

Until now, you have focused strictly on the numbers game, and it has served you well to weed out poor product choices. Now you need to bring some cognitive evaluation into this process by using the Product Evaluation Test.

Product Evaluation Test (Column J)

Choosing the right products for your eBay business is not strictly a numbers game. Additional factors are at play that are not always revealed in raw numbers.

Once you have found the products that meet your minimum margin and profit requirements (check marks in columns H and I of Spreadsheet #3), you should review each of them against other important factors to be sure you will not make a product purchase (for resale) mistake. The Product Evaluation Test is based primarily on your intuition about the product, which may come from the research you performed. Consider the following factors in product evaluation.

Fads. Is that hot item you are looking at selling a solid product choice for your business or just a fad? You can capitalize on fads and make quick money. However, I would not want to build a business around a fad. Does this product meet your future business plan? If it is a fad you can still sell it, but don't depend on it as a long-term product and don't stock a lot of it in your inventory.

General or Specialty Product. Are you a general product seller or a specialty or niche seller? If you are a specialty or niche seller, does the product fit your product line? You don't want to confuse your customers with unrelated items if you have a specialty store. If the product doesn't fit your product line, you can sell it through another eBay account, or you should skip it. Note that you can have as many eBay accounts as you need, but each must have a different e-mail address and credit card.

***SEE ALSO* Chapter 2, "General Market vs. Specialty Market"**

Product's Strategic Purpose. Why do you want to sell this product? What will be its strategic purpose? Later in the book we will explore bait products and store inventory products. A bait product is an auction listing placed on eBay to draw the maximum number of hits. Then within the bait product's description, buyers are sent to your store to purchase other items from your store inventory.

***SEE ALSO* Chapter 9, "Determine Your Bait Products"**

Is This Product Bait or Store? Is it possibly not even strategic to your business, but a product you may want to list as a standalone? Each listing type can work, but you need to clearly understand why you want to add this product to your line and how you will use it. Will this product be a good addition to your product line or confuse your customers? If you have no clear reason why you want to sell this item or see no strategic value, you may want to find better prospects.

Physical Product Size. How large is the item? Products that are large, heavy, or unusually shaped can be difficult and costly to ship (both to you and by you). While I would not rule out a big money-making product that is oversized, I would discourage you from adding this product if you can sell other items with the same profit margin that are easier to handle and ship. For example, compare selling a grandfather clock versus an expensive watch. Both will bring top dollar and tell time, but the watch is much easier to ship.

Product Cost. Is the cost of the item prohibitive? If you sell a $1,000 item but your cost is $700, stocking only 10 of these will set you back $7,000. Can your business afford this? Probably not when you are just starting out.

SEE ALSO **Chapter 12, "Managing Your Inventory"**

Prohibited, Restricted, or Recalled. Make sure that your item can be sold on eBay. You cannot sell prohibited or recalled items. If there are restrictions, be sure you understand those restrictions before you purchase anything for resale.

If your product has passed these evaluations, you should place a check mark in column J (Passed Product Evaluation Tests).

#3. Profitability Worksheet Analysis

The final step in your methodology is to identify the products that have passed all of your tests. Therefore, if a product has a check mark in columns H (Profit), I (Margin), and J (Product Evaluation), then place one last check mark in column K, **Passed All Tests.** In our sample worksheets, only the Sony DVD player and the Black and Decker leaf blower passed all of our tests.

If the product missed your profit requirements, then the product has failed your test and is not a product you should attempt to sell on eBay at this time. If your product passed your profit requirement but failed your margin requirement, you can choose to pass on that item or conduct further, deeper analysis.

Sometimes, even when a product fails the margin requirements, you will have a strong feeling that you could still sell the product successfully on eBay. Maybe you think you can beat your giant competitors and turn all those red prices into green. In these cases, our methodology does allow for further analysis. If, however, you used HammerTap and Instant Market Research to conduct your analysis and the product failed their tests, forget about that item for now. Don't fight the data no matter how much you want to sell that product. Make product decisions based on profit, not on emotion.

Methodology Conclusions

All products on your #3. Product Profitability Worksheet that have a check mark in column K, **Passed All Tests,** qualify as a product that you should definitely consider selling on eBay. You have just found the products that provide the best chance for success and should choose your products from this list. You have found your gold nuggets!

Special attention should be given to any products in column K that also have checks in the small **Ideal Niche** or **<20** checkboxes. You may have just found a gold mine!

Just think of what you have done. Here are the highlights of what you have accomplished so far with your methodology. You have ...

- Investigated product ideas from high-quality sources that have the best probability for success.

- Sifted through your product list to eliminate poor performers and found the products with the highest demand and lowest competition.

- Conducted a profitability analysis on the remaining products in order to ensure that they will be not only profitable, but profitable enough for you to bother selling.

- Generated a list of products that are proven to have a high success rate on eBay. You can now select the products you want to sell from this list of guaranteed winners.

#3. Product Profitability Worksheet

List all qualified products from Worksheet #1. or #2. Use two lines if necessary.

Your minimum Profit Margin Requirement is ___25%___ *(25% is suggested)*

Your minimum Profit Requirement is ___$10___ *($10 is suggested)*

A. Product Name	B. Avg. Selling Price (ASP)	C. Retail MSRP (Manuf. Website)	D. Est. Cost (C × 50%)	E. eBay and PayPal Fees (B × Fee%)	F. Profit B − (D + E)	G. Margin% (F ÷ B) × 100	H. Meets Min. Profit	I. Meets Min. Margin	J. Passed Product Eval. Test ✓	K. Passed All Tests ✓ □ I. Niche □ < 20
Sony DVD Player FX820	$125	$154	$77	$8.75	$39.25	31%	✓	✓	✓	□ I.N. □ < 20
B&D Hedge Hog Trim	$64	Outlet Mall on Sale	$45	$5.12	$13.88	22%	✓			□ I.N. □ < 20
B&D Blower BV2500	$56	Liquidator	$14	$4.48	$37.52	67%	✓	✓	✓	□ I.N. □ < 20

Your Gold Nuggets!

Wait, I Don't Have Many (Any) Products That Qualified!

You may be disappointed to discover that few or maybe even none of your products passed all the tests. I understand your frustration that a lot of effort did not produce any approved products. But what if you hadn't done this research before you purchased those products? You have just saved yourself hundreds or possibly thousands of dollars, a garage full of unprofitable items, and the cost of a case of Rolaids.

Some days the old gold prospector came up empty, too. That didn't mean he should quit or that his equipment didn't work. It meant he was panning in the wrong part of the river that day. So were you.

If you have conducted your product research methodology only to discover that the items were not profitable, don't force it; simply move on. Don't be discouraged. This methodology is working for you. Go back to your #1. Product Idea Worksheet. What other categories are you interested in exploring? Start the process over again in other categories, searching for completely different products.

Keep in mind that this process becomes simple once you know the methodology. The time and effort to conduct product research and analysis will always give you the advantage. Be encouraged that you have the methodology that will save you from the mistakes that many eBay sellers are making. In fact, you know more about product selection and analysis right now than 98 percent of all eBay sellers—including PowerSellers!

Now move on to explore new products, categories, and giants. You will find the category with the profitable items. It may just be the next item, niche, giant, or category you research. The reward is well worth the work because you will only be selling items that are already proven to be profitable!

Find Reputable Product Suppliers

Popular sources of products for eBay sellers include flea markets or garage and estate sales. However, those products, although legitimate, are one-shot opportunities and, therefore, not at all what this book is about. To build a solid and dependable business, you need product sources that are more reliable. You used a solid methodology to find your products, so now you will continue the methodology to find reputable, consistent, and enduring suppliers of those products.

The good news is that the tough work is over. You have found the products you want to sell on eBay. You can relax a bit, but just for a little while because now we need to find reputable suppliers for your products.

In this chapter, we will examine how the supply chain works and the differences between the various suppliers. If you have decided to general sell, then most likely your products will come from liquidators, surplus sellers, and other similar sources. If you will specialty or niche sell, then your suppliers will mostly be wholesalers, drop shippers, and importers.

From Manufacturer to Consumer: The Distribution Supply Chain

Before we proceed to find our suppliers, it is a good idea to understand the different types. This will help you see where you, as an eBay seller, fit in the distribution supply chain. We will start with manufacturers and end with the consumer.

There are always exceptions to the standard supply chain method. However, manufacturers do not usually sell products directly to consumers. That is not how their business is organized. When was the last time you spent an afternoon shopping at a manufacturing plant?

Manufacturers can be both domestic and international. The vast majority of products sold on eBay are produced outside the United States. Manufacturers create a product either for their own company or for other companies under a private label.

The eBay Seller's Supply Chain

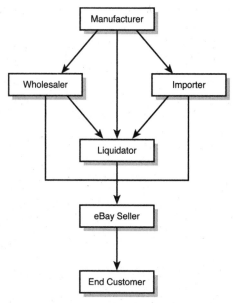

The eBay Seller's Supply Chain

A manufacturer is set up to create, produce, sell, and ship large quantities of product. The volume produced is usually too sizable to ship even to retailers unless they are very large chains. Small retailers cannot handle the storage, much less the cost.

Many large retail chains have their own warehouses. Manufacturers will ship directly to them, sometimes producing private label products for a retailer. In those cases, the wholesaler is removed from the supply chain, but that is the exception.

Most manufacturers ship large amounts of their products to wholesalers, not retailers. Large-volume wholesalers have huge warehouses to store all of their products. Most specialize in supplying products to particular retail markets. Retailers then purchase products from the wholesalers in smaller, more manageable, and affordable quantities.

When manufacturers, wholesalers, and large retail chains decide that a product needs to be replaced by a newer model, should be repackaged, or the season has changed (clothing, bedding, sporting goods), they may choose to liquidate. Surplus products are sometimes liquidated by the wholesalers and retailers directly, but most of the time these products are sold to large-volume, online liquidators.

Secondary market retailers, including online Internet website and eBay sellers, visit online liquidator sites looking for extreme discounts on popular, brand-name products. There are several good categories on eBay in which to sell secondary market products.

This entire process, from manufacturer to end consumer, is called the distribution supply chain. It is important to understand how it works, where your products will come from, and where your eBay business fits in the chain.

Wholesalers

Wholesalers purchase their products from manufacturers in large quantities and sell them in lesser quantities to retailers. There is no standard markup from the manufacturers for their products because each industry and marketplace is very different. What is fairly common, however, is the cost to retailers. Most wholesalers charge retailers about 40 to 60 percent off the manufacturer's suggested retail price (MSRP) for their products. Retailers, in turn, usually double their cost to determine their retail price to the end consumer.

Therefore, since everyone needs to make a profit, there are three separate markups along the distribution supply chain: the manufacturer's markup, the wholesaler's markup, and the retailer's markup. Everything is based on the original price from the manufacturer. If a similar product can be produced much cheaper by another manufacturer, then the end price is also significantly reduced for the consumer. This explains why so many products are manufactured overseas.

EBay sellers who specialty or niche sell usually purchase their products from wholesalers. There are actually a variety of wholesalers such as distributors, light-bulk wholesalers, importers, and drop shippers. We will examine the differences between these types.

Distributors

A distributor is a smaller wholesaler that usually employs a sales staff for you to work with. They tend to specialize in one or just a few markets. Distributors usually allow smaller minimum order quantities than the larger wholesalers. (See the section "Light-Bulk Wholesalers" later in this chapter.) Distributor prices are usually a bit higher than from larger wholesalers. The process they use to distribute their products to retailers is about the same as wholesalers. For the discussion in this book, consider the terms wholesaler and distributor to mean the same thing.

Light-Bulk Wholesalers

Light-bulk wholesalers, a term coined by Worldwide Brands, stock less inventory and will sell to you in smaller quantity minimum orders. You should seek light-bulk wholesalers for products that have good demand but not enough to require you to stock significant quantities.

You may pay a bit more for your products, but you also don't have to purchase so much that it sits in your garage for months before it is sold. That ties up your money and, therefore, is not good inventory budget management.

Drop Ship Wholesalers

Some wholesalers will actually ship a single product directly to your customer for you. These are usually distributors who have expanded their wholesale business to include drop shipping. Most charge either higher prices or a small fee per package for this service, but there are some that do not.

There is an enormous advantage for online sellers when using drop shippers. Your inventory cost is zero! You don't stock inventory. Instead, you sell directly from the drop shipper's inventory. This method gives your inventory budget enormous leverage and can take your business from the beginner phase to professional in a matter of weeks.

SEE ALSO **Chapter 10, "Are You Ready for Drop Shipping?"**

Liquidation Wholesalers

Manufacturers, wholesalers, and retailers use liquidation wholesalers (liquidators) to eliminate older models, closeouts, discontinued items, or overstock items from their inventory. Many online liquidators sell their items in "lots," meaning several of the same item or several of a variety of items.

Some of their items will be new and in factory-sealed boxes. Other items will be refurbished units, defective units, or customer returns. The bill of lading (BOL) is always viewable from reputable liquidators so you know the exact condition of the particular products that they are selling.

Some liquidators sell items at a fixed price, while others have auction sites much like eBay. Liquidators will require you to purchase the entire lot of items, and they don't allow returns. So it is important that you are dealing with a reputable liquidator and not just one you discovered on the Internet. (See the section "Finding Reputable Liquidators" later in this chapter.)

The biggest advantage of liquidators over wholesalers is that you can purchase new, in-the-box, factory-sealed products at a very small fraction of the MSRP. This is where you will achieve outstanding profit margins.

SEE ALSO **Chapter 5, "Minimum Profit Margin"**

The problem, however, is that you are usually purchasing several hundred items in a lot. They will be delivered to you on pallets. Do you have room to store them? Moving your wife's car from the garage to the driveway in January when you live in Minnesota is not the solution.

Purchasing items from liquidators is a reason why your methodology is so important. Before you place a bid on that "lot" of items, conduct product research on eBay to ensure that you can sell them individually and profitably. You want to look at the sell-through rate and the average selling price.

This is why I recommend using HammerTap. When you discover an appealing product from a liquidation auction, use HammerTap and do a Quick Search. In less than a minute, you will know whether the product is worth considering or not. It either fails the test immediately and you move on, or it passes the test and is worthy of further analysis on your #3. Product Profitability Worksheet. You have a pass/fail decision in seconds. Yes, seconds.

SEE ALSO   **Appendix B, "How to Use HammerTap"**

Large-Volume Wholesalers

Large-volume wholesalers stock a lot of inventory. They usually require a minimum order quantity that is much larger than distributors or light-bulk wholesalers. The advantage of using them is that they also provide a volume discount on their products.

You want to search for a large-volume wholesaler if you have found a product with very high demand on eBay. Instead of purchasing small quantities, you may want to purchase in volume and benefit from the deeper discount.

Import Wholesalers

Import wholesalers (importers) purchase huge quantities of items from overseas (mostly Asian) manufacturers. The biggest advantage is that you can purchase newly manufactured products from importers at prices that are much lower than other wholesalers.

The disadvantage is that you have to place a large order to meet an importer's minimum quantity. Do you have the budget, and do you have the room? Most of all, is the demand on eBay high enough to justify the volume purchase?

If you would like more information about working with importers, check the website www.globalsources.com. It has several resources and reports you can purchase that explain how the import process works. Also check www.globaledge.msu.edu and click on the **resource**

desk page. Other helpful sites are www.busytrade.com and www.
rusbiz.com.

Finding Reputable Suppliers

Here's a fun test. Conduct an Internet search using the keywords
"wholesaler," "liquidator," or "drop shipper." You will receive tens or
even hundreds of thousands of hits. Then include the keyword "eBay,"
and it gets peculiar.

Here come all the unbelievable ads. "We are the single source for all
your eBay product needs!" Well, lucky you. These guys can do it all,
eh? When anyone claims you can buy all of your eBay products from
them or through them, forget about it. They are middlemen and you
need to run away fast.

Middlemen

Middlemen pose as wholesalers or drop shippers, but in reality they
are retailers. They take orders from you, go to their suppliers, order
the same products you could get on your own, and then have them
drop shipped to you. The problem is that you are being overcharged
from the middlemen. In most cases, their markup is so high that their
products won't generate any profit on eBay.

There is a second problem with middlemen. You can only buy the
goodies that they have in their basket. This is exactly opposite to the
way you should find a supplier.

Don't select your products only from their basket and then go and try
to sell them on eBay. You will have enormous competition because all
their other members are doing the same thing with the same products.
That is guaranteed to be a losing proposition.

You have already learned from your methodology that you find the
products that are profitable on eBay first and then you locate the suppliers of that product. The chance that those products will be supplied
by a middleman is rare if ever. See the difference?

Legitimate wholesalers, drop shippers, and other suppliers rarely
advertise on the Internet. They do not take advantage of an amateur
seller, but are looking only to establish a business relationship with

serious online sellers. Therefore, you will not find your suppliers by conducting random Internet searches.

Find Reputable Wholesalers

The way to avoid middlemen and other Internet scams is to not use the Internet to search randomly for your suppliers. There are much better methods. The first method is to contact the manufacturer directly.

When you were completing your #1. Product Idea Worksheet, there was a column you should have completed if you knew the manufacturer of the product. Many times the manufacturer's website or contact information is printed on the back of the item's package or in the magazine advertisement. You need to refer to that information now and transfer it to your #4. Product Supplier Worksheet (see the "Working with a Wholesaler" section later in this chapter).

If you don't have that information, go to Thomas Register at www.thomasnet.com. Thomas Register has free information concerning almost every medium to large manufacturer in the United States. You just enter the keywords of the product, and Thomas Register will provide you the name of any company that manufactures or supplies that product.

Once you have found the manufacturer, call them. (Don't send an e-mail unless they do not supply a phone number.) All you need to say is that you are an online seller and want to carry several of their products. Ask them who the wholesaler is for your area. You have just found a legitimate wholesaler.

Finding Reputable Liquidators

I recommend a different method for finding reputable liquidators. It is by using the member sites What Do I Sell® and Worldwide Brands. Both of these companies were introduced earlier in this book, and you will now see even more reasons why I recommend them.

What Do I Sell®

Lisa Suttora, the founder of What Do I Sell ®, is the trending expert I recommended in Chapter 4 to find the hottest, new products and trends on eBay. Fortunately, her website also maintains and provides access to several databases of reputable suppliers, wholesalers, and liquidators.

Lisa actually started her site in order to answer the questions that all eBay sellers have:

"What do I sell?"

"How can I get those products from reputable sources?"

I used to spend 80 percent of my time searching for legitimate sources of products before I discovered What Do I Sell®. In order to be listed in her approved supplier databases, a supplier must pass an in-depth and rigorous analysis by Lisa and her staff. For every 40 suppliers that apply to her site, only 1 will be approved.

The scrubbing of suppliers that Lisa and her staff perform cannot be duplicated by an eBay seller on his or her own. It is entirely too time-consuming. Therefore, I pay my monthly fee to become a member of her site. The small monthly fee is minimal because it eliminates 80 percent of my product sourcing work.

What Do I Sell®
Supplier Links

Membership to What Do I Sell® includes not only access to reputable supplier links but to her product trending analysis newsletters. She also holds a conference call every month so her subscribers can call in to hear and view her presentation online. Each month has a theme of either product sourcing or trending. At the end of her presentation, she entertains questions from her members. This is your opportunity to ask her any product trending or sourcing question or to get help with any problem you have.

Now I will let you in on one of my PowerSeller secrets. I go to Lisa's site routinely to find links to her approved liquidators. I then click through to the liquidator's site and scroll through all its products being liquidated. When I find an item of interest, I pull up Hammer-Tap, perform a Quick Search analysis, and I can determine in about one minute whether the item is worth pursuing.

Lisa allows eBay students to receive a membership that is substantially discounted from her standard rates by using the link www.whatdoisell. com/studentrate. Note again that your discount is not shown until you use this link and then click to purchase her Business Premium package. Then scroll to the bottom of the checkout page to see her generous discount.

Worldwide Brands

Worldwide Brands (WWB) produces the Instant Market Research Internet analysis tools. Membership to its site also comes with another bonus—access to its databases of reputable product suppliers.

SEE ALSO **Chapter 3, "Worldwide Brands's Product Sourcing Membership"**

Online sellers use WWB to find the different types of wholesalers mentioned earlier in this chapter. Of particular interest, however, is its database of reputable drop shippers.

Using their research tools, you can find reputable suppliers for many of your products. In order to qualify for inclusion in the databases, suppliers must also go through a thorough investigation similar to Lisa's site. These are the types of suppliers for which WWB maintains databases:

- Drop ship wholesalers
- Liquidation wholesalers
- Instant import buys (importers)

- Light-bulk wholesalers

- Large-volume wholesalers

It is important that you know that neither Worldwide Brands nor What Do I Sell® is a middleman. On the contrary, you use these two sites specifically to avoid middlemen and go directly to the reputable suppliers. You buy no products from either site. They are merely the gatekeepers that I use and recommend to find reputable suppliers.

Whenever I need to find a supplier, I go to these two sites first. The suppliers listed on their sites are expecting you and want to do business with you. You can even complete and submit a dealer application to suppliers directly from WWB's site. If I cannot find a supplier by checking WDIS or WWB first, only then do I resort to Thomas Register to contact the manufacturer.

Note that not all suppliers listed in WWB's databases will sell to eBay sellers. In these cases, this is stated upfront so you don't bother sending an application to them. Just move on to another listed supplier.

Worldwide Brands's Product Sourcing Membership program includes the drop shipper database, all of its other supplier databases, and its Internet analysis tools. They also offer an excellent training program as an optional upgrade called the Whole$ale eBiz Education. If you can afford to add this upgrade to their standard membership, by all means take advantage of their training program and discount. The company offers a discounted lifetime membership at www.worldwidebrands.com/studentrate.

Working with a Wholesaler

So you have found the best supplier for your product—what's next? Now you need to apply for a dealer application. When you are getting started, you will be ordering several products from many suppliers. In order to organize this process, use the #4. Product Supplier Worksheet.

If you have Instant Market Research, you can complete the dealer application online. To find suppliers with Instant Market Research, conduct a Product Search and click the **Supplier** tab. You will see a list of reputable suppliers for your product.

SEE ALSO **Appendix A, "Analyze a Product"**

#4. Product Supplier Worksheet

List all qualified products from #3; transfer contact info from your #1. Product Idea Worksheet or from Instant Market Research.

Your Approved Product	Supplier Contact Information (name, phone, website, e-mail)	Type of Supplier (Wholesaler, Light Bulk, Drop Shipper, Liquidator, etc.)	Dealer App. Requested	Dealer App. Sent	Supplier Interview Completed	Product Ordered
B&D Blower BV2500	bestliquidators.com 800-555-4444 ext. 512 Courtney	Liquidator	✓	✓	✓	✓
			✓	✓		

#4. Product Supplier Worksheet

The suppliers will be listed, such as light-bulk wholesalers and drop shippers, as well as the number of suppliers for each type. If you click the **number** link, you will then find the actual suppliers. Clicking on the supplier will provide you with contact information including a dealer application. Complete the application and submit it.

If you have found suppliers on your own, then you will need to contact them to request a dealer application. Wholesalers are major businesses. It is vital that you are well prepared and businesslike. You don't call and chit chat about the weather. In particular, don't ask what products they have that would be good to sell on eBay. You would just have identified yourself as a "newbie" and an amateur.

Keep your discussions short and all business. Speak with confidence. When you talk about your business use "we" instead of "I," such as "We want to carry your products." That is how businesspeople talk. You simply say, "We are an online retailer and want to carry many of your products. I am calling to request a dealer application." That is basically it.

They may ask you a few questions to weed out the amateurs, such as your website or business license tax ID. Have all of this information in front of you when you call. Note that it is best not to have an e-mail address with your name; you should have a business sounding e-mail address. For example, thetreasurechest@comcast.net is a much better-looking e-mail address than janedoe@yahoo.com.

SEE ALSO **Chapter 12, "Get Your Business License"**

If they ask for your website, state that you are an eBay seller. If you have an eBay Store, give them the URL (Internet address) of your store. Then wait for the response. In most cases, that will be acceptable. Wholesalers have learned that legitimate businesses sell on eBay. You just need to convince them that you are a legitimate business. Your business license should do just that.

If they ask you for your fax number and you don't have one, ask if they can just scan it and e-mail it to you. Don't tell them to send it to your local Kinko's. It quickly identifies you as small-time. If they can't e-mail it, then have it mailed.

Once you have asked for a dealer application from a wholesaler, place a check mark in the column **Dealer Application Requested** on worksheet #4.

Complete the Dealer Application

Once you get your dealership application, be sure to fill it out completely. Some new sellers are stumped by the references portion of the application. Use as a reference anyone you have conducted business with, including CPAs, an attorney, or even the company that prints your business checks.

Sometimes the credit references are only needed if you are applying to purchase your items on credit (net 30 days). If you plan to pay for your items with a credit or debit card (I use my PayPal debit card), the reference section is usually waived.

Once you have sent your dealer application, place a check mark in the column labeled **Dealer Application Sent.** It usually takes about two weeks to be notified of approval status.

Wholesaler Interview Checklist

Once you are approved, you will most likely be assigned to one of the wholesaler's salespeople. Contact the person right away to introduce yourself and discuss the company's procedures and requirements so you can get started.

Once again, you need to be prepared. Have your questions already written down and in front of you when you call. For a start, here are some of the questions you will need to ask:

- How do I place my orders (phone, e-mail, online ordering system)?
- What are your minimum order requirements?
- What are your payment terms (credit card, on credit for net 30 days)?
- How will you ship the items to me?
- Do you ship internationally?

- How do you handle returns for damaged or nonworking products?

- Whom do I contact if there is a problem?

If this is a drop ship wholesaler, ask how it will handle returns from your customers. Eventually, you should also ask the salesperson about the minimum in-stock quantities that they consider should be in stock for your products so you will not have the dilemma of selling out-of-stock items.

SEE ALSO **Chapter 10, "The Drop Shipper Inventory Checklist"**

Sometimes you may have wholesalers tell you it is okay to sell their products on eBay, but that you must sell them at a fixed price and never below 15 percent off the MSRP (retail price). Great, you were just accepted and will be able to order and sell those products!

Occasionally you will find that certain products cannot be sold on eBay. Some manufactures will not allow their products to be sold on eBay or even online. If that is the case, forget about it. Don't fight the system, no matter how much you want to sell that product. You are wasting your time. There are plenty of other products to sell.

After you have completed your interview with the wholesaler's salesperson, place a check mark in the column **Interview Completed.** You are now ready to order your products!

Ordering Your Products

Once you are dealer approved, you will be able to order your products. There may be several different ways to place an order, depending on the wholesaler's system. If the wholesaler is large, it may have an online ordering system. It will provide you with a login and password to enter the system. You will order your products by product name or the part number that the wholesaler uses for its inventory.

If you are using a drop shipper, all you have to do is change the delivery address from yours to your customer's. The wholesaler will charge your credit card, and the fulfillment center will ship the product to your customer.

If the wholesaler does not have an online ordering system, you will use the phone, an e-mail, or fax. If you order by phone, I suggest you always follow up with an e-mail as a hard copy record of your order. This way, if there are any problems with the order such as wrong product, color, or size, you have proof of what you ordered.

Once you have ordered your product, place a check mark in the final column of the #4. worksheet, **Product Ordered.** Congratulations! Your methodology has taken your original product idea through a complete profitability analysis, to dealer approval, and now to the fulfillment and satisfaction of actually placing an order for that very product.

Listing Techniques and Strategies

So far in our methodology, you have accomplished the tough work of extensive research to find only profitable products. We will now examine the best practices that top PowerSellers use for creating professional, successful listings. You will once again not use any guess-work when creating your listings. Instead, you can base all of your listing-creation decisions on solid evidence and then use only the specific techniques and tweaking that will increase the selling price of your particular item.

Before you list any item on eBay, some prep work is required. First, take a photo(s) of the item to be sold in order to insert it into your listing. You will also need to weigh the item in the shipping box, along with all packing materials, to help determine how much you are going to charge for shipping. Finally, it will be necessary to determine the answers to many questions in order to complete the listing form. To determine those answers, you will need to find the top sellers of your product and study how they create their listings. This process is called "eBay research."

This chapter will equip you with the best listing techniques and strategies that you should use when creating your listing. We will begin with our prep work, then cover listing creation, and finally discuss advanced listing strategies. Using these methods, you will be one of the top sellers for your product the first time you list it.

Take Professional-Looking Photos

Your gallery picture is one of the most important factors that differentiates you from your competition. Many times the picture alone will attract buyers to your listing. I cannot state this any clearer: if you want to attract the most attention to your listings and bring top dollar for your items, you need professional-looking gallery photos. This is especially true if you sell in the jewelry, collectibles, or antiques categories.

The gallery photo will initially attract buyers to your listing. Once the buyer is viewing your listing, if the layout, description, and additional photos look professional, so will you. With all other components being equal between you and your competitor (price, shipping, description, and so on), if your listing has the best-looking photos, your item is the one they will want.

Spend some time experimenting with and learning how to use your camera properly. Obtain professional yet affordable photography equipment and learn some photography methods, tips, and tricks from the professionals. If eBay is your business, then photography is a big part of your job. Consider taking a digital photography course at your local community college or community center.

Photography Tips for Great-Looking Photos

In my book *eBay Business at Your Fingertips*, I cover photography techniques and equipment extensively. Some of that information is summarized here.

Backgrounds. Choose an appropriate background for the item. In many cases, white is the best background. Use inexpensive backgrounds such as poster boards, butcher paper, white (ironed) sheets or a few samples of different colored fabric. Photography stores carry background rolls much like wallpaper rolls. Determine the best background for the item by holding it up next to the cloth. Whichever background contrasts nicely with the item and makes it look the most three dimensional is the best background to choose.

Lighting. There is no such thing as too much indirect light. Light brings out the texture, color, and character of the object. Adjust the quality of the light and diminish glare with diffusers and reflector cards.

Flash. Turn off the camera's flash and use side lighting instead. Use fluorescent, "balanced" daylight bulbs (the ones shaped like a corkscrew).

Natural light. On an overcast day, move your photography stand out to the patio. Natural light will also bring out the true colors of your item, but avoid direct sunlight. The best arrangement is outdoor photography that is in the shade.

White balance. Make sure your camera has been "white balanced" after each setup and just before you take your pictures so that your camera will capture the true colors of the item (refer to your owner's manual). Don't ignore this step. This is one of the most important steps in digital photography. It can be the difference between an off-color picture and a photo with true colors.

Cleanliness. Wipe the item clean before taking the pictures to remove lint, smudges, and fingerprints. Wipe your camera lens clean with an approved lens cloth.

Right side up. To help keep items upright (that would normally roll or fall over), use a small beanbag underneath the background cloth or a pink pearl eraser behind the object. You can also use museum wax, gel, or putty as long as it does not leave residue on the object.

Macro. Use the macro setting for small objects or items about the size of a remote control and smaller.

Tripod. Always use a tripod to avoid shakes when you take the picture, and also to keep your setup the same for multiple pictures. Use the image stabilization feature if your camera is equipped with it. Otherwise, consider using the timer or a remote switch (shutter release cable) so you do not need to touch the camera when the picture is taken.

Reflections. Watch for unwanted reflections on shiny surfaces. They can usually be removed with diffusers. Attach the diffusers to the lamp and cover the bulb. For an inexpensive diffuser, you can even use a white sheet. Be careful that your bulb is not hot or the sheet can catch fire. This is why I use florescent bulbs.

Pedestals. For small collectibles, construct a "pedestal" by placing a box or, even better, a Quaker Oats cylinder container under a genuine velvet backdrop and place your object on top. This creates a point of focus for smaller objects. It also gives an impression of greater value.

Photography Equipment

If you are selling ordinary, inexpensive items that you are getting rid of, then a basic photography setup will probably produce adequate pictures for eBay. However, if you sell collectibles, expensive items, or want exceptional product photos to beat your competition, then I suggest investing in professional-quality yet affordable photography equipment.

Popular photography equipment for eBay sellers are cubes, cocoons, and tents. These are all collapsible, fold-up enclosures made of light-diffusing material. You place your item in the all white cube and position the lights on each side. Light is then diffused onto the item through the cube. These enclosures solve two problems: the need to diffuse the light and a white background (some light tents come with multiple backgrounds for items that need a different color).

Cloud Cube (top), and the Cloud Dome (bottom)

If you sell small items such as jewelry, coins, gems, minerals, stamps, comic books, or other items that lay flat, consider the Cloud Dome. It was actually designed for use in the forensic industry and has made a few appearances on the *CSI: Crime Scene Investigation* TV show. EBay and Internet sellers have also discovered the Cloud Dome, and it has grown in popularity because of the even light diffusion and the excellent images it produces, even in low light.

The dome is made of high-impact, crack-resistant plastic. The camera mounts on the top of the dome. The light spreads evenly on the object, creating a dispersion with no shadows or hot spots.

Determine the Shipping Rate

When you create your listing, you will need to determine your shipping rate. You can either charge a flat rate to all buyers or let eBay charge a calculated rate that is based on the buyer's zip code.

Arguments can be made for and against both methods. What I have chosen to do is to charge a flat rate to all 48 states if a package weighs less than 5 pounds. For packages over that weight, I believe it is not fair to charge the same rate to a customer who lives nearby that I would to a customer who lives across the country. So, for items over 5 pounds, I use the calculated rate.

To determine the proper weight, you will need a postal scale. It is not a postage meter but a scale. You will use it to weigh the item in its shipping box along with all packing materials. You then note the weight for use later when you create the shipping rate section of your listing.

One of the more popular postal scales that eBay sellers use is the UltraShip. It has a digital readout that can display lbs/oz or kg/g. It also has several useful features, such as auto hold and zero reset, used to determine tare weights. The best feature is that the front panel display can be removed from the scale and moved out more than 1 foot. This is especially handy when weighing boxes that are large and would cover the readout.

The UltraShip 55-pound scale should serve all of your eBay shipping needs from small packages weighing a few ounces up to 55 pounds. It has more features and is a lower price than competing scales available from office-supply stores or even the U.S. Postal Service.

UltraShip Postal Scale

You should be aware that these scales are being used as a source of fraudulent activity online, including on eBay. Unscrupulous sellers pose as authorized dealers, advertise the genuine product at a reduced rate, and then ship a cheap knockoff. It is for this reason that I carry the genuine scales in my eBay Store just for my students and readers at www.trainingu4auctions.net.

Answer Your Listing Questions

There are over 50,000 categories and subcategories of products on eBay. No one can be an expert in all of them. Even an eBay professional is most likely only an expert in about a dozen categories. Using our methodology, however, you can sell an item that you have never sold before—and have very limited knowledge of that category on eBay—and still receive the highest bids for your product. The way you accomplish this is by conducting proper eBay research.

Every listing you create on eBay will require you to answer the following questions:

- What listing format should I use?

- In what category should I list my item?

- What should my starting price be?
- What keywords should I use?
- What should I say in my descriptions?
- When should I start my listing?
- Which listing duration should I use?
- Will listing enhancements or upgrades increase the price for this item?

Most sellers guess at the answers to these questions. Each incorrect answer will diminish their listing's outcome. There is no reason to guess when all the answers are readily available through eBay research.

eBay Research

You will now find the top sellers of your selected item, study how they created their listings, mimic their techniques and strategies, and expect the same success rate they enjoy.

select **Completed listings**

Search Completed Listings

Step 1. Find the Top Sellers

Use the following steps to find the top sellers of your product on eBay for the last two weeks:

1. From eBay's homepage, select the **Advanced Search** link on the quick search bar.

2. In the **Enter Keyword or Item Number** search box, type the primary keywords that you would use as a buyer to find the item you are about to list and click **Search.**

3. You will now see a list of all items currently for sale on eBay that include those keywords in their title.

4. Narrow the list down to the specific item by adding more keywords, or eliminate certain keywords by typing them in the **Exclude these words** field from the Advanced Search page.

5. Once you have narrowed the search to the specific item you want to sell, you will see all the items currently for sale on eBay that match those keywords.

6. Now scroll down the left side under Search Options and Show Only. Click the checkbox **Completed Listings** and then click **Show Items.**

7. Now you will see all the items that match the keywords for your item that have completed (ended) on eBay during the last two weeks. The prices in green mean those items sold for that price. The prices in red mean those items did not sell.

8. Toward the top right of the screen, click on the **Sort by** drop-down box and select **Price: Highest First.**

You now are reviewing all of the listings for your type of item that have received the highest bids in the last two weeks. All listings that have the highest green prices are the best performers. Therefore, you have found the top-performing listings of that item for the last two weeks.

Step 2. Study Their Listings

Now that you have found the top sellers, your next step is to study how they listed the item so that you can answer your listing questions. There is a form I have developed for recording your findings during this step called Top Seller Listing Analysis. It is available for download along with your Product Notebook worksheets at www. trainingu4auctions.com/notebook.

Top Seller Analysis Form

Seller Used ID: _____

Keywords: _____

_____

_____

Category/Subcategories: _____

_____

Starting Bid: _____ Reserve: _____ BIN: _____

☐ Auction-Style ☐ Fixed Price Price Sold: _____

Duration Days: ☐ 1 ☐ 3 ☐ 5 ☐ 7 ☐ 10 ☐ 30

Ending Day: ☐ Su ☐ M ☐ Tu ☐ W ☐ Th ☐ F ☐ Sa

Ending Time: _____ ☐A.M. ☐P.M. PST

Number of Photos: _____ Number of Hits: _____

Enhancements: ☐ Subtitle ☐ Bold ☐ Border

☐ Highlight ☐ Other: _____

Description Benefits/Features to Include: _____

_____

HammerTap: ASP_____ LSR _____ ☐ Ideal Niche

OneSource: Marketplace Research Results _____ %

Pass/Fail : Demand ☐ P ☐ F Competition ☐ P ☐ F

Best Supplier: _____

☐ Drop Shipper ☐ Light Bulk ☐ Liquidator ☐ Other

Top Seller Listing Analysis Form

Open the top 10 or more listings (only the ones with green prices, meaning the items sold) and study how the top sellers listed the item. You want to look in particular for the most important elements of success, such as the following:

- What were the title keywords they used?
- In which category did they list the item?
- What was their starting bid?
- Did they use a reserve price?
- Was it an Auction-Style or Fixed Price listing?
- Did they use a Buy It Now price?
- How detailed was their description?
- How many photos did they use?
- How many days did they run their auction?
- What day of the week and time did the listing end?
- How many hits did their auction attract? (Look at the bottom of the listing for the hit counter. Note that sometimes the counter is hidden by the seller.)
- Is there anything special about their description that you may want to include?

You need to create a separate analysis sheet for each top seller, merge your findings, and purge the poorer choices. For example, if 7 of 10 top sellers use an Auction-Style format, you will use Auction-Style when you create your listing. If 7 of 10 top sellers use a starting price under $10, start your listing under $10, and so on. When you have finished your analysis, you will have the answers to the questions that arise when creating your listing.

Expect that conducting this analysis manually, even for one, will take 20 to 30 minutes when conducted properly. While this is fine if you sell just a few items per week, it can take a lot of time if you are a serious seller and list many new items per week. You should know that HammerTap can conduct all of this analysis for you with 90 days of search data and can provide the answers to all your listing creation questions in about 10 seconds.

SEE ALSO **Appendix B, "Detailed eBay Market Research"**

What if You Can't Find Your Item on eBay?

Sometimes the eBay research method will produce no listing titles that had the keywords for the item you were researching. Remember that when using a completed listing search, eBay is only allowing you to look back in history for 14 days. Therefore, it is very likely that rare or collectible items may not have sold on eBay in the last two weeks.

When this happens to me for rare or collectible items, I prefer to conduct research on the most popular antique sites. I then search for my item on www.goantiques.com and www.tias.com. If you have several antiques or collectibles to sell, consider joining www.priceminer.com. For a very reasonable monthly rate, you can use their tool to search the antique websites. Simply enter the keywords of your collectible, and PriceMiner will scour up to 10 years of historical information looking for all sales of your item.

If you find that the information for your item is not conclusive, then determine in the best way you can what you think the value is and set a reserve price for that amount. If your item is not rare or a collectible but did not show up in a completed listing search, try to broaden your search by adjusting your keywords slightly. If you still cannot find the item, try www.pricegrabber.com, www.amazon.com, www.shopping.yahoo.com, www.froogle.com, and sometimes www.overstock.com. Otherwise, conduct Internet searches to find the product, similar products, or websites with similar products.

If you have Instant Market Research, conduct a Product Search using the Analyze a Product methods and click the **Advertising** tab. You should be able to find your major Internet competitors using this method.

SEE ALSO **Appendix A, "Quick Analysis"**

Create Professional Listings

There are certain techniques you should also incorporate during listing creation that will substantially increase the number of browsers attracted to your item. More browsers mean more bidders, which will result in a higher final sale price. This next section will show you how to create professional listings to maximize your sales.

Which Listing Type to Use

You have two choices of listing types for standard auctions: Auction-Style and Fixed Price. The most commonly used is Auction-Style. However, the percentage of Fixed Price listings is growing every year. This indicates that more advanced sellers are moving to Fixed Price.

Used and personal items are usually sold using the Auction-Style format. The item is offered at auction, and buyers place bids on the item. Whoever the high bidder is when the auction ends wins the item.

Fixed Price listings are offered for one predetermined price only. There is no bidding involved. Either a buyer will purchase the item at that price during the listing's duration, or it will remain unsold.

These two methods are totally different approaches to selling a product. One may be very successful, while the other may go the entire listing duration with no buyers. So which method should you use?

Follow your research. Whatever method the top sellers of this item are using to bring the highest selling price is the method you should choose. Also check to see if the top sellers are using a combination of formats such as Auction-Style with a Buy It Now option, or maybe even a Best Offer format.

When to Use a Reserve

Sellers who list items at auction sometimes want to include a reserve price in order to protect their listing from ending at too low a price. Consider a reserve price the minimum amount you are willing to accept for the item.

If a reserve is used in a listing, a link titled "Reserve not met" will appear directly below the current price. As bidding progresses and then meets or exceeds the reserve, the link will change to read "Reserve met."

Reserve prices are strictly optional to the seller, and the actual price is hidden from buyers. It is entirely up to you whether you want to reveal the price in your description. If you use a reserve, expect a few e-mails asking you what the price is. It is your choice whether to reveal it or keep it hidden.

EBay charges a fee to protect your listing with a reserve price. The reserve fees are as follows:

Reserve Price	Fee
$0.01 to $199.99	$2.00
$200 and up	1% of reserve (up to $50)

From a marketing perspective, reserve prices usually should not be used. Buyers tend to stay away from them. So if you use a reserve, you will be discouraging buyers from bidding on your item. So when should you use a reserve price?

Your research will tell you if it is warranted. If your research shows that the item's average selling price has been holding steady for the amount you want (or better), then you should not use a reserve. If, however, the selling price has been erratic, many times selling for much less than you want, you should use a reserve. I also suggest you use a reserve on very expensive items, collectibles, and antiques. Buyers of these items expect reserves (just as they would if they were buying in-person from a major auction house).

Never use a Fixed Price listing for an antique or collectible. You do not want to limit the amount that someone may be willing to bid for these items.

Find the Best Keywords

Keywords are the single most important component for a successful eBay listing. Searching keywords is how 80 percent or more of your buyers will find your listing. You want to spend considerable time searching for and developing the proper keyword string that will become your listing's title.

In our methodology, when you get to this step, you have already completed your eBay research for the particular item. The best keywords that you discovered from the top sellers will be the primary keywords you should use. However, before you stop with your keyword analysis, I suggest you perform one more step.

Use powerful keyword finder tools, available from Internet search engines, to help you locate the most searched keywords buyers use when they search for your item on the Internet. These are the keyword finding tools I recommend:

- http://keyword.ebay.com

- https://adwords.google.com/select/KeywordToolExternal

- www.wordtracker.com

- http://tinyurl.com/58y7c5 (Yahoo! Keyword Finder)

Combine any outstanding keywords you have found using these tools with the keywords from the top sellers. EBay limits the number or characters in the title to just 55, and all characters count, including spaces and punctuation. Therefore, you will need to pare all your keywords to the select few that you think will draw the most hits and not exceed 55 characters.

A basic mistake new sellers make is to treat their listing title like advertising copy. This is a mistake. Save your advertising copy for your description. The title you use should strictly be made up of the best keywords that buyers will use to find your item. Trust your research, use only your carefully determined keywords, and then narrow them down.

Because all characters count, do not use any unnecessary punctuation. You are not writing a sentence, and it does not even matter what order you write your keywords in order to obtain search hits. You should, however, arrange them in the most logical way from left to right to make it as readable and understandable as possible. The keywords are not case sensitive, but I suggest to not type in ALL CAPS; instead, use Mixed Case. If you need a particular keyword to stand out from the others, type only that word in all caps. Always double-check your spelling.

If your item is new, I suggest you squeeze in one more keyword: "NEW." Many buyers who only want new items will narrow their search by using "new." I would type "NEW" in all caps and make it the first word in the title.

Be sure you do not keyword spam. Some sellers add keywords to their title that are not relevant to the item they are selling but are very popular on eBay. For example, maybe they are selling a thermos but want to increase their hits so they include words in their title such as iPod and LCD TV. Sellers caught doing this will have their listing cancelled, and their listing fees will not be returned. Continuing this practice will result in account suspension.

If you have HammerTap, see the steps on the research process in Appendix B. This will show you the keywords that have proven most successful in increasing the price for your particular item on eBay in the last 90 days. This is invaluable information when you need to limit your keywords, and this is not something you can determine on your own without a powerful analysis tool.

SEE ALSO **Appendix B, "Category Search"**

Write an Ideal Description

Your description is the advertisement for your item. Therefore, you should write your description much like detailed advertising copy you see in magazines, newspapers, and online. I don't mean that your description should consist of a bunch of headlines. You should have just one very strong advertising headline at the top of the description page and then the name of your item on a separate line just below your headline.

You want to spend some time developing a good headline. Buyers have very short attention spans, and a poor headline makes them reach for the mouse. A great advertising headline encourages them to stay and read more. Check the top sellers for their headlines, and then search the Internet for sellers of the same product. Don't make the headline exactly the same as your competitors'. Just study them all and then create your own. I suggest that you use larger type and a different font for your headline than your description. Also consider using a different color, perhaps royal blue or navy. Don't make it too bright or a faded color. Red looks like a stop sign. Blue is inviting.

When you study the top sellers of your item, read their descriptions. You are not looking to copy the description; you are mostly looking to see if you have left any important feature, fact, or benefit out of your description. Don't go on and on with several paragraphs for a common item that everyone knows.

The main goal in your description is to answer the questions that buyers will need to have answered before they even want to place a bid. Therefore, view it from the buyer's vantage point when you write your description and use the following questions as your outline.

For all items:

- What is the item for sale?
- What does the listing include? Is it just the item or are accessories or giveaways included?
- What are the item's color, size, weight, and dimensions?
- What is the item's condition?

For antiques and collectibles, also mention the following:

- Who made it? Where and when it was made? Include any unusual history, if known.
- Is it autographed or a numbered edition?

For more technical items, give the following details:

- Make, manufacturer, model number
- Technical specifications
- Warranty status

In your policies section, state the following:

- The shipping and handling rate and shipping method you will use
- Your payment policies
- Your guarantee and return policies

The body of your description should be in black and white. Leave the color to the headline. Keep your background white because colored backgrounds sometimes make the text hard to read. I suggest using

Arial or Times New Roman fonts for the body. Limit bolding words to only those that need special attention.

DO NOT WRITE IN ALL CAPS! DO YOU SEE HOW HARD THIS IS TO READ when compared to reading this? Writing in all caps is also considered shouting when written online. You don't want to shout at your potential customers.

Your paragraphs should be a maximum of two or three sentences. Use proper grammar and punctuation. Always use a spelling checker when you have finished writing.

Choose the Best Day and Time

There are good days and times to end an eBay auction, and there are bad times. Many sellers never realize this. They end their listings at 3 A.M. and wonder why they have such lousy results.

Why isn't your local shopping mall open at 3 A.M.? Because all of their shoppers are in bed. So why would an eBay seller end a listing at that time? If you think it doesn't matter because buyers can place a bid at any time, then you are definitely a new seller.

Experienced sellers (and buyers) have learned that the vast majority of bids will be placed in the last few minutes of the auction. This creates a huge spike in the number of bids at the end of your listing duration. In order to get the biggest spike, you must end your listing when the vast majority of your buyers are free and have the availability of a computer.

The consensus now among eBay PowerSellers is that Sunday nights between 5 P.M. and 7 P.M. PST is the best day and time to end an auction for general items. Most people are free Sunday nights and 7:00 P.M. PST is still only 10 P.M. EST.

This rule of thumb is not true for all items and categories, however. If you sell items that businesspeople would be interested in, they are not normally on eBay looking for these items on the weekend. Stay-at-home moms may be very busy on Sunday nights and freer during the weekdays. Some sellers of popular products like to end their auctions on Monday. The reasoning is that they are catching the losing bidders from Sunday, when there is less competition. How do you know when to end the listing for your item? Your research will provide the answer.

Be sure when creating your listing that you use the "schedule" feature so you can kick off your listings at an appropriate time and so they will end on the best day and at the time you desire. This is one of the more helpful listing options that eBay provides. It gives flexibility for you to list your item when you have time and have the listing begin at a later time and date.

If you do not have HammerTap, I suggest you list ordinary items so they will end Sunday evenings unless your research tells you differently. If you are a HammerTap subscriber, you can perform a Product Search, and the report will tell you which day and time will produce the highest average selling price for your specific item.

Determine the Best Starting Price

Starting prices can begin at 1 cent or be as high as you want. Your insertion fee is based on the starting price. The starting price insertion fees can be found on eBay by clicking the **Help** link, then typing **eBay.com fees** in the search box. You can also get a quick calculation estimate by using www.ebcalc.com.

When examining the fees, it is clear why so many listings on eBay start under $1. Sometimes this is quite acceptable. I have sold many items on eBay that I started at 99 cents, and the final price was several hundred dollars. However, this does not always work. You could very well list your item for 99 cents and have it end with just one bid of 99 cents.

This is, again, why we depend on our research to give us the answer. Whatever the starting price is that the top sellers have been using successfully is the starting price you want to use.

Charge a Reasonable Shipping Rate

The shipping rate you charge has a direct relationship to a buyer's impression of your trustworthiness. A shipping and handling rate should cost your buyer no more than the amount to ship the item plus a reasonable charge for handling and shipping materials (no more than about $2).

Sellers who attempt to make a sizeable profit from their shipping rates are not providing good customer service. It is very easy for a buyer to compare the shipping rates of competing sellers. It is also very easy for a buyer to give you a poor shipping price rating in your feedback Detailed Seller Ratings (DSRs). The correct approach used to this point to attract your buyers will not matter if you try to gouge them with a high shipping rate and have a poor DSR feedback rating on your shipping price.

When you visit almost any website to purchase an item, have you noticed how reasonable the shipping rates usually are? Why do you think that is? It is because professional retailers don't overcharge their customers with excessive shipping rates. In fact, many now offer free shipping on orders over a specific amount. This is a very hot button for many people, and you should not push it either.

A typical eBay buyer usually analyzes a listing and makes a bid/pass decision in this order:

1. Is this the item I want?
2. Is it in acceptable condition?
3. Is that a price I am willing to pay?
4. Is the shipping and handling rate reasonable?
5. Is the seller's feedback good?
6. Are the return policies fair?
7. Does the seller accept PayPal?
8. Sold!

If any of these components are out of line, buyers will decide to click off of your listing and move on to your competitor in about five seconds. Do not risk losing sales just to make a few dollars more on shipping.

Instead, use the buyer's decision analysis to your favor. When you present a reasonable shipping rate, you look better to the buyer than your competitor. The buyer may even be willing to bid a higher price for your item because everything about your listing, particularly the fair shipping rate, created a favorable first and lasting impression.

When to Use Enhancements

Enhancements, also referred to as listing upgrades, should occasionally be used to give more visibility to your item. The Bold, Border, and Highlight enhancements are the most often chosen listing upgrades. Changing your listing title from standard type to Bold will make it stand out from the others. A Border places a box around the title. Highlight enhances the listing with a colored background similar to using a highlighter in a book.

Enhancements can be expensive, so be sure that they are cost effective if you continue to use them. The eBay fees for these listing enhancements are:

$1.00	Bold
$3.00	Border
$5.00	Highlight

Venture out occasionally and try something new. Always track and measure the success of your listings when using enhancements and compare them to the results of your standard listings.

Note that it is nearly impossible to predetermine the success of enhancements when conducting manual eBay research. I always use HammerTap for this purpose.

When to Use Subtitles

A good use of subtitles would be when you want to have an important message noticed such as "Free Shipping for Buy it Now" or "We Ship Worldwide!" or mentioning a "freebie."

If you are selling a popular product that has significant competition, consider including a free item that does not cost much but will give added appeal or benefit. For example, if you are selling $75 binoculars, include an inexpensive compass or a lens cleaning cloth. Then use a subtitle such as "Includes FREE Compass!" Your item is now the better deal for your customers, and they will be attracted to your listing. Subtitle fees are 50 cents, so don't use them on inexpensive items.

Golden Rule Payment and Return Policies

You will need to write your payment and return policies in your listing. Don't take this step lightly. It is part of the buyer's pass or bid decision questions mentioned earlier. If all else looks good with your listing but you have demanding or intolerant policies, your buyer is gone.

Think of the Golden Rule and write your payment and return policies like those you would prefer to see if you were the buyer. Which policy would appeal more: "No refunds or returns. All sales final!" or "100% Money Back Guarantee!" Convince your buyer that you are committed to customer service and their complete satisfaction. Think Nordstrom's, not pawn shop.

Policies that are firm, fair, and friendly will actually help convince buyers that you are experienced and someone they would want to deal with. You will give the assurance that if something should go wrong, you will stand behind your product. You then become their low-risk and high-quality choice.

Advanced Listing Techniques and Strategies

Sometimes I think eBay sellers make sheep look like independent thinkers. Have you ever browsed through a category on eBay and noticed that nearly every Gallery Picture was the same stock photo from the manufacturer's website? No listing stands out from any other. If you were a buyer, how would you decide which item(s) to study further? What would motivate you to click on one listing over another? It would be the one that is somehow different from all the rest. This can be accomplished mostly with photos, subtitles, listing upgrades, and enhancements.

Good advice for stock market investing is to be the contrarian. Whatever the crowd is doing, you do the opposite. I use the same strategy in dealing with my competition on eBay. My listings stand out from my competitors' because of the differences. I may use different photos, pricing, enhancements, or anything that catches the eye of potential buyers so that they want to click on my listings instead of my competitors'.

Contrarian Gallery Pictures

When a buyer conducts a keyword search that matches, your listing will appear in the search results along with all of your competition. Your item may be clearly visible among a few results or lost among many. As buyers scan the listings on the results page, they are looking for something that stands out. They begin scanning the photos, pricing, shipping, title, and subtitle looking for a reason to select one listing over the other. You need to give them a reason to pick yours.

Study your competitor's listings and then mix it up a bit. Take a picture of your item with a different background, format, or angle. Keep your pictures professional quality and make them just different enough to be noticed. For example, if other sellers are displaying the same picture of the unit, take a picture of the box.

Consider Using Auctiva

Many eBay sellers use Auctiva to receive free scheduling and discounts on other eBay enhancements. One of the free features of Auctiva is the ability to cross-promote your listings. The tool scrolls gallery pictures of your other listings at the bottom of your listings. Many buyers will view these pictures, click on them, and view another of your listings. Learn more at www.auctiva.com.

Insert a Billboard Instead of a Photo

I learned this next trick from Mike Enos, a Platinum PowerSeller. If you want to be completely different, you can set yourself apart from your competition by creating a message such as "Free Shipping" or "We Ship Worldwide" in Microsoft Paint and then substituting that message in place of your gallery photo. Use the gallery photo space as a billboard instead of a picture. Buyers are attracted to the billboard. Once they click on your listing, they will then see the product photo that you have inserted as a second picture.

Experiment with this technique by using a different message each time. Track the sales results to determine if this method is indeed increasing the final sales price and then adjust accordingly to the one that is working best. If you see no increase in sales for the item you are selling, go back to a gallery photo instead of using a billboard.

Use Misspelled Keywords

You can purposely use misspelled keywords in your bait listings in order to get more hits. What? Are you serious, Kevin? You bet I am!

Honestly, just how well do you spell? Even if you won the spelling bee, would you agree there are many buyers that are poor spellers? If you only use keywords that are spelled correctly for products that are commonly misspelled, your listings will not appear on a search from all those buyers who can't spell. However, if you sell items that are commonly misspelled, list the correct spelling as well as the incorrect spelling, and you will capture both types of customers!

You may think this makes you look "dumb" as many of my students have said. I tell them that I don't care if I look dumb if I get more money for my listings and beat my competition. However, if this bothers you, here's a tip so you look like you actually know how to spell. I suggest you lay out your keywords in your listing title as follows:

correct keyword, other keywords, misspelled keyword

By placing the correctly spelled keyword at the front and the misspelled keyword at the end of your title, you have shown that you actually do know how to spell—if that matters to you. Believe me, it doesn't matter one bit to my buyers or to me.

However, I know this will be hard for many of you because you don't know how words are commonly misspelled. My sister, Cindy, is one of them. She has been a medical transcriptionist for many years. She can effortlessly spell medical terms correctly that I cannot even begin to pronounce. If you are like my sister, then you probably have no idea how certain words are commonly misspelled. I have help for you.

Go to www.typobid.com. You can then type the correct spelling of a word, and this site will show you the most common misspellings of that word.

Following are some examples of a few commonly misspelled keywords used on eBay.

Hummingbird	Humminbird
Diamonds	Dimonds
Earrings	Earings
Pittsburgh	Pittsburg
Canon camera	Cannon
Cuisinart	Cusinart
Brett Favre	Bret Farve

Look at the first set of words. Which is correct, Hummingbird or Humminbird? Well, if you are selling bird feeders, Hummingbird is correct. However, if you are selling fish finders, Humminbird (without the "g") is the correct product name.

If a fisherman tells his wife he wants a new Humminbird fish finder for Father's Day, what spelling do you think she will use to find it on eBay? The one with the "g"—which is wrong! If you are the seller and you only spelled the product brand name correctly (with no "g"), your listing will not show up on her eBay search. You lost that potential sale!

How many men do you think know how to spell Cuisinart? It starts with a "Q" doesn't it? Would you agree that many nonfootball fans don't know how to spell Brett Favre? Is a Canon camera with one "n" or two? It does not matter if you can spell correctly. What matters is that many of your customers will have typos in their search keywords, and you need to adjust your titles in order to catch them.

Do you see now that if you don't include commonly misspelled words, especially brand names, you are losing a lot of potential buyers? Remember, I am only talking about the commonly misspelled keywords to use in addition to your correctly spelled keywords. You want to capture both types of buyers, those who can spell and those who can't.

Add Interactive Video

I recently discovered a company that provides interactive video that you can insert into your listings. I have been most impressed with their product. It has increased the number of hits, bids, and sales for the sellers who are using it.

Using professional actors, they have created a variety of interactive video clips that communicate with the buyer and help encourage him to bid. Say you have a Best Offer listing. As a buyer is viewing your listing, an actor walks into the screen and begins talking. The actor encourages the buyer to place a bid and will continue to communicate with him throughout the bidding process. The discussion changes based on what the bidder does. You can also choose from a variety of characters in order to portray the mood you want to convey in your listing—from businesslike to humorous.

For sellers who use this feature, the results have been excellent. I think buyers enjoy coming back to these listings. It has brought the fun back to buying on eBay.

It is very simple (nontechnical) to add their videos to your listings. The company also offers a very reasonable payment plan whereby you initially deposit a small amount to begin and they will deduct a small fee each time you use their technology in one of your listings. Note the fee is based on one listing, not the number of times it is viewed.

To experience these fun interactive videos, and for a free trial, go to www.deal4it.com/studentrate and click **View a Demo.**

Keep an Eye on Your Competition

Now keep an eye on your competition. They are watching you. When they realize what you are doing and see the success you are having using these advanced strategies, they will begin to use them as well. When they do, go back to the original method.

Many times I have created successful "product packages" that sold very well for a certain period of time. Once my competition caught on to what I was doing, they started offering the same thing. As soon as they did, I went back to selling the items separately. Buyers who were interested only in a particular individual product were again buying from me.

Be the contrarian. Change things around and do just enough to set yourself apart from your competition, whether it is with photos, subtitles, shipping, product packaging, or some other method. Customers will be attracted to your listings instead of the competitors' because you have designed a different look that creates interest and catches their attention.

8 Provide Superior Customer Service

Have you ever had a doctor, accountant, attorney, or other professional (or even his or her staff) who was competent but rude, condescending, or discourteous? Were the person's abilities overshadowed by his or her behavior? Did you end up finding another professional? What about that new restaurant where the food was good but the wait staff was inattentive and not at all courteous? What was your overall impression? How small was your tip? Will you ever go back?

One of the foremost aspects of excellent customer service for any business is the opportunity to attract valued repeat customers. Careless packaging, delayed shipping, and a lack of any personal attention or appreciation can be a deterrent to repeat eBay business, and can seriously lower your Detailed Seller Ratings (part of your feedback). You must provide service that is superior to your competition.

Let's examine your competition in order to first understand and then surpass them. Typical eBay sellers (your competition) ship their items by UPS or USPS Parcel Post. Often they may wait two or three days after payment before they get around to shipping the item. This means that eBay buyers become accustomed to receiving their items one to two weeks after they have paid. In addition, many eBay sellers provide no thank you note or marketing information in the package. They may never even contact their customer again.

Some eBay sellers do not bother to leave feedback for their customer, or they do so reluctantly only after being reminded. You can excel in each of these areas, receive wonderful feedback, and gain a multi-purchase returning customer for the life of your business simply by correcting each mistake listed previously.

- Leave positive feedback as soon as the buyer pays you.

- Include a "thank you" letter, a PayPal packing slip, and other marketing materials with each order.

- Pack the item professionally and ship the item by the next business day.

- Ship as many items as practical using USPS Priority Mail (two- to three-day deliveries) and the eBay/USPS co-branded Priority Mail boxes.

- Send an e-mail notification with the delivery confirmation tracking number when the item is shipped so that the customer knows when to expect it.

- Solve any problems quickly and fairly. The emphasis should be on customer satisfaction.

Leave Feedback

When you are starting your eBay business, you will need to make time in your process to leave feedback for your customers. If you don't bother to leave feedback for them, what incentive do they have to leave glowing feedback for you? Try to accomplish this at least every other day, or the list will grow to be a chore.

As your business grows and you are selling several items a week, the feedback requirement can become unmanageable, and you may tend to avoid it. You can get help and automate this process for just $15.99 a month using Selling Manager Pro.

When you are ready for this service, upgrade your eBay account by purchasing Selling Manager Pro. You will find many tools with this application that can help manage your eBay business such as inventory management, automated e-mails, and automated feedback.

Simply open your My eBay page and, under the Selling Manager Pro section, select and set your preferences to leave feedback automatically whenever a buyer pays you with PayPal. You can customize the feedback message that you want eBay to leave for your customers.

When a buyer pays you with PayPal, eBay will now automatically leave feedback for your customer. A great benefit of this feature is that positive feedback is left for your buyer immediately after he or she pays for your item. Most customers will notice this and greatly appreciate it.

Judy's Treasures
P.O. Box #
City, State, Zip Code
www.judystreasures.com

{Hand write: *Hello Customer's First Name,*}

Thank you for your purchase! All of our products have been carefully chosen, are of the highest quality, and are offered at excellent prices for you, our valued customer.

We trust that you will be completely satisfied with your purchase. If there are any problems, please let me know right away.

I have already left great feedback for you. If all is as you expected, please leave great feedback for me as well. Thank you!

If you would like to be notified about our special sales and promotions, please go to my eBay store at www.judystreasures.com and select the link "Sign up for Store newsletter." Be assured we will never share your information and you can unsubscribe from our customer mailing list at any time.

Enjoy your new purchase!

Best Wishes,

Judy

Judy A. Seller
President
Judy's Treasures, LLC

eBay Store: www.judystreasures.com
email: judy@judystreasures.com

Thank You Letter

You have just eliminated your feedback routine. Believe me, if you are moving a lot of items and can eliminate your manual feedback task, the $15.99 a month is a bargain. Learn more about Selling Manager Pro at http://pages.ebay.com/selling_manager_pro.

Advertise Your Business in Every Package

Before you seal any package, why not promote your business by including your business card, pens with your eBay Store's web address, or perhaps discount coupons for the customer's next purchase? Your coupon could be 10 to 15 percent off or maybe free shipping on the next order over a certain amount.

An excellent way to set yourself apart from your competition, market your business, and be viewed as an eBay professional is to include a "thank you" letter in each package. In your letter, state that if customers would like to receive e-mail notifications from you when you offer specials, they should go to your eBay Store and select the **Sign up for Store newsletter** link. Now you can send e-mail campaigns every few weeks to announce sales and special promotions.

SEE ALSO **Chapter 9, "Send Newsletters to Your Customers"**

Use Free USPS/eBay Co-Branded Boxes

EBay has partnered with the United States Postal Service to provide co-branded Priority Mail shipping boxes. The boxes are printed with phrases such as "Buy it on eBay, Ship it with the U.S. Postal Service" or "A Preferred Shipping Service on eBay." Shipping your items in these boxes gives a professional presentation. Your customer will also be pleased with such a quick delivery time.

The boxes come in different sizes for both variable rate (based on weight and destination) and flat rate (same rate no matter the weight or destination). You can order each box size in quantities of 10 or 25 once every day.

You must use these boxes for Priority Mail shipments only. Certainly not every item you sell on eBay needs to be shipped by Priority Mail. Small, lightweight items under 1 pound can be sent First Class.

Larger items will require you to supply your own corrugated box and possibly use Parcel Post or UPS rather than Priority Mail. For items between 1 and 4 pounds that can fit in the free boxes, using Priority Mail makes good business sense.

USPS/eBay Priority Mail Boxes

If you priced equivalent-size boxes from an office-supply store, they would cost about $2 to $5. If you have a part-time eBay business and sell four items a day, that is $240 to $600 a month just in boxes. That is a giant bite out of your monthly profit.

Priority Mail packages can be delivered anywhere in the continental United States in two or three days. Although this time frame is not guaranteed, it is usually met. The price difference between a package that weighs under 4 pounds using Priority Mail, as compared to Parcel Post, is only about $2 more depending on destination. Not only will you charge your customer this difference, you can actually make a statement in your shipping policies, "We ship by Priority Mail!" Most customers prefer a quicker shipment as long as the additional charge is minimal.

Your buyer will leave feedback for you using Detailed Seller Ratings (DSRs). One of the ratings is for shipping time. Most buyers are sensitive to the length of time it takes from purchasing the product to final delivery. A high DSR score is also used by eBay to give priority placement to that seller's items during Best Match search rankings. I receive terrific scores and feedback comments about my speedy delivery. My high DSR score then helps my items receive higher rankings during search results. It is all because I use Priority Mail.

The benefits of significant cost savings, two-day deliveries, a professional presentation, and high DSR scores using the co-branded boxes makes choosing Priority Mail an excellent customer service decision. You can order the co-branded boxes from http://ebaysupplies.usps. com. There is no charge for the boxes and no charge for delivering them to you.

Other Corrugated Boxes and Packing Materials

Not all of your items can fit in the co-branded Priority Mail boxes. Therefore, you will also have need for your own corrugated boxes. Keep in mind the impression you will make with your customer by the type of box you use and how the item is packed. I do not normally recommend reusing shipping boxes unless they are still in very good condition. The box should not have any tears, holes, or damaged corners. All shipping labels should also be removed. The box should appear as new, not reused.

Since you cannot depend on having boxes to reuse, I recommend that you find a reasonably priced source of corrugated boxes. Conduct an Internet search for corrugated box companies near your location.

The particular box company I use is Uline at www.uline.com. It has an exhaustive catalog of different-sized and -shaped boxes and should be able to meet your shipping needs. Its prices are much lower than what you would pay at an office-supply store. You can also receive quantity discount rates with volume purchases of 50 or 100 boxes. Uline has strategic locations around the nation, allowing for quick delivery and lower transportation costs.

You don't always have to pay for your packing materials. Many local merchants would be happy for you to take their Styrofoam peanuts, paper packaging, and bubble wrap. Furniture stores in particular have excesses of these materials. Determine what you need and ask your local merchants if they would be willing to provide it to you at little or no charge. What a beneficial way to recycle. If you need to purchase packing materials, I recommend www.uline.com, www.papermart.com, www.fast-pack.com, and don't forget about eBay!

Ship Quickly

A hot button with buyers is the amount of time it takes to receive their item. Don't ignore this important component of your customer service. It can be a determining factor for the type of feedback you will receive from your buyer.

If possible, always ship by the next business day after the payment is made. This is very simple to accomplish when you incorporate the steps of printing prepaid postage and using home pickup as part of your fulfillment process.

Remember not to print any postage or ship any package until you have been paid by the customer. PayPal will send you an e-mail notice of payment. Once you have received the payment, you can print prepaid postage from your home computer.

Print Prepaid Postage

print prepaid shipping

To print prepaid postage, follow these steps:

1. Go to your My eBay page and click on the **Sold** page. Select the **Print Shipping Label** link under the Action column for the item that was paid. You will be redirected to your PayPal account where you will need to log in.

2. On the PayPal shipping page, choose your carrier (USPS or UPS), choose the shipping service type, and enter the package dimensions and weight. Under Shipment Options, choose the mailing date (choose the next business day) and any optional services you require such as insurance.

3. Choose the **Continue** button and review the summary page to be sure all information is correct. You can now print the prepaid postage and a packing slip. Attach the shipping label to your packages with clear packing tape.

You can also choose the link to request carrier pickup from your home. Choose a pickup for the next business day. Note that UPS charges for home pickup, and the United States Postal Service will pickup packages at no charge as long as at least one is a Priority Mail package.

On the morning scheduled for pickup, place your items on your porch or in another area you have designated. That is all there is to it. No more trips to the post office!

Send an E-Mail Shipment Notice

Customers are curious about what is happening on your end of the transaction. They just paid for their item and may be a bit anxious about when they can expect to receive it.

If you use the aforementioned prepaid postage method, PayPal will automatically send an e-mail to your buyer telling him or her that the postage was printed. This is an efficient, time-saving service. Note, however, that PayPal sends the e-mail when you print the postage, not when you ship the package. So don't print postage several days before you plan to ship, or your customer will assume it is already on the way and then wonder why it hasn't arrived (pay particular attention to printing postage on weekends and holidays so you don't accidentally do this).

If you do not use the prepaid service, then as a courtesy to your customer send an e-mail notifying him or her of shipment. Be sure to include a tracking number if you have one. This creates anticipation for the item's arrival. It is an excellent and important step of your customer service. USPS Delivery Confirmation is free if you print your postage online, and most experienced buyers expect to receive that number within a day or so of paying you.

Handling Shipping Problems

Although shipping problems are rare, they do occur. You can expect them as part of an eBay business. I have found that most buyers are honest. If they have contacted me to complain about a late delivery or damaged items, I believe them.

Always respond quickly to resolve the problem. The way you handle problems determines the feedback and DSR scores you will receive. Most buyers are reasonable and understand that sometimes things can go wrong. Use the Golden Rule and handle the situation professionally, the way you would expect if you were the buyer.

Many times a late package will still arrive if given another day or two of patience. Explain this in an e-mail to your customer. Most of the time when the package arrives, the buyer will see that you shipped it quickly, realize that the delay was not your fault, and still give you good feedback.

If the item was damaged and you can replace it from additional stock, do so as soon as the buyer ships the item back to you. If the item was a one-of-a-kind item and you cannot replace it, have the buyer ship it back to you for a full refund including the shipping cost.

Never take advantage of a customer even when you can. Conduct your business and resolve problems with honesty and integrity. Incorporate factors that enhance your buyer's experience and continue to conduct your eBay business in this manner. Your commitment to customer service will reinforce your buyers' trust in you. A satisfied customer is a returning customer.

Open Your eBay Store

One of the better strategies for maximizing your profits on eBay is to list regular Auction-Style listings in conjunction with related listings in an eBay Store. Not only do you sell your auction items, but many of your buyers will visit your eBay Store where you have other items available for purchase.

Why Open an eBay Store?

An eBay Store is very similar to a website. It is your own page(s) on eBay where you can list all of your items together in one organized and attractive presentation. It is essentially an online catalog of all your products, giving a much more professional image of your business to your buyers.

An excellent reason to open an eBay Store is that buyers who are attracted to your listings can click a link within your listing that will forward them directly to your eBay Store. In your store, you will stock related items such as accessories, and give quantity discounts. The buyer can also view all of your other items and possibly make an impulse buy. This creates upsell and add-on selling opportunities.

Another advantage of an eBay Store is to save money on listing fees. The Insertion Fees for store inventory items are only 3 cents for store items priced under $24.99, 5 cents for $25.00 to $199.99, and 10 cents for items $200.00 and above. Compare those fees to the Insertion Fee to list an item on eBay using the Auction-Style format. Plus, you can have a quantity of 1,000 of any particular item, and the listing fee is still only 3 to 10 cents.

Store inventory items also have a longer listing duration than standard auctions. While 10-day listings are the longest duration for a standard auction, your store items will be listed for 30 days (same as Fixed Price listings). You can also request that your items be renewed every 30 days if they have not sold. This is especially helpful when selling several quantities of one product. Create one listing in your store, select the quantity, and choose your listing to renew every 30 days using a Good 'Til Cancelled (GTC) option. Your listing will remain in your store, renewing every 30 days until it has sold out. EBay will adjust the quantity that appears in your listing as the item sells until the quantity is exhausted.

Open an eBay Store

If you go on vacation, you can use your store's vacation mode to manage sales. This allows you to leave your items visible and available for purchase, but a banner will read that you will ship when you return. You can also easily close your store while you are away and make your items disappear. Upon return, you open your store again and all the items reappear. Note that your subscription fee will continue even if your store is closed.

Store Subscription Levels

There are three monthly subscription levels for eBay Stores: Basic, Premium, and Anchor. For your first store, I suggest you choose the Basic level for $15.95 per month. You can always upgrade later once your volume of sales justifies the cost.

Basic Store, $15.95. This is the most appropriate choice for casual or part-time sellers. Included in the subscription is an unlimited number of product listings, five fully customizable catalog pages, tools to help you create and manage special promotion newsletters that can be e-mailed to a maximum of 5,000 subscribers, a subscription to Selling Manager, and phone support staffed by eBay customer representatives.

Premium Store, $49.95. This level is for serious to full-time eBay sellers. All of the features of the Basic store are included in this package plus an upgrade to 10 catalog pages and 7,500 subscriber e-mails. In addition, Premium stores include a free subscription to other eBay tools such as Selling Manager Pro, eBay Marketplace Research, a discount on Picture Manager, and more advanced store traffic analysis reports.

Anchor Store, $299.95. This subscription is only for eBay professionals with a large business operation. Anchor stores have all the features of Basic and Premium plus 10,000 subscriber e-mails, 15 catalog pages, and a free subscription to Picture Manager.

Your total store fees then are the monthly subscription, the Insertion Fees when initially listing the store items, and the Final Value Fees when a store item sells. To learn more, select the **Help** link on eBay, then type **eBay Store fees** in the search box.

When to Open a Store

An eBay Store is not necessary for every seller. If you are new to eBay or sell only a few items per month, you do not need a store. If you are a serious seller, then using our product analysis methodology, you will want to open your store once you have found and determined only your profitable products. At that point, you will be able to determine which products should be sold using standard listings and which products should be in your store inventory.

If you have not yet completed this part of the methodology, it is difficult to justify the cost of a store. Casual sellers, selling used and unrelated items, will receive little benefit from displaying them in a store. It would be the same as going to a website or opening a catalog and seeing a few scattered, unrelated items. The effect this would have on your customers would be the opposite of what you want. They would not be very impressed and less likely to purchase anything. When you are in that beginning phase of selling, just use standard eBay listings.

You want your store to be a showcase for all your items. You can select among several custom designs to create themes. A store should be fully stocked with many appealing items so that, when buyers land on your store, it will create a great first impression. They should want to browse.

Once you have determined your product line using our methodology, you need to determine what the most popular and enticing items will be. These will be your "bait" products. You list these items as Auction-Style listings to draw customers to your listings. You then send them to your store.

How to Open and Design a Store

EBay has developed design tools to make the setup of your store simple. To open an eBay Store, click on the **Stores** link just below the keyword search field, at the top of eBay's homepage. You can use the basic templates eBay provides or use advanced design tools to produce a more customized layout.

Design your store as you would a website. I suggest you look at websites and eBay Stores that sell the same products you will sell. Study their descriptions, titles, layout, and categories.

Design Your eBay Store

You will use categories in your store to organize your products rather than have them all listed together. Create categories based on the products you will be selling. You can have up to 300 categories, but try to keep the number to about 25 or less. Any more than this and your store starts to become jumbled. If you are selling so many products that you need more than 25 categories, you may need more than one store.

Choose a design theme appropriate for the items that you sell. Use varied styles, colors, and graphics to give it a different look than your competitors. If you have a logo, you can insert it in your store design. Logos can cost a few hundred dollars if designed by a graphic artist. However, you can find simple-to-use logo-design software on the Internet or at office-supply, electronics, and computer stores.

Set Up Your Store to Receive Internet Searches

So many sellers, even PowerSellers, have not set up their stores to maximize searches from buyers that originate outside of eBay. This is a big mistake because many eBay buyers actually start their original search on the Internet.

How many times have you searched the Internet for an item and then seen the link on the right of the screen that says, "Find this item on eBay"? You want to use and properly place carefully chosen keywords throughout your store in order to receive search engine optimization (SEO) from the major Internet search engines.

A common mistake that eBay storeowners make is that they have written their store title, description, and categories as if they are writing an advertisement. The secret to properly setting up your store for SEO is to use keywords just as you do when creating your listing's title.

You should not write ad copy; you should use searchable keywords that Internet buyers will use and that Internet search engines will recognize. When the buyer types one of those keywords, Google or other search engines will respond with "Find this item on eBay." The buyer clicks on that link, and they just landed on the list of stores that have the item, including yours.

Here's how to optimize your keywords to give you a higher rating from the Internet search engines:

1. Select your **My eBay** tab.

2. Under My Subscriptions, select **Manage My Store.**

3. Under Store Design, select **Search Engine Keywords.**

4. You now see all your primary and secondary keywords used in your store front page categories. Edit your keywords for SEO as explained here:

   - **Store Front Page, Primary:** Don't use your User ID for your store name's primary keywords. Place the most important keywords there. Instead, insert a logo in the place provided to display your store name.

   - **Store Front Page, Secondary:** This is your store description. Include the major brand names of all the items that you carry. Use singular words like "clock," not "clocks," so you can get as many keywords as possible in your description. You can only have up to 300 characters, so use them wisely.

   - **Store Category, Primary:** Use meaningful keywords that an Internet searcher would use yet that still describe that category. For example, use "Fish Finders," not "Marine Electronics." A person would be much more likely to search for "Fish Finders" than they would to use a broad term like "Marine Electronics." Yet "Fish Finders" can still be a category if you sell several models. Use plurals in your category keywords since there will be more than one item in each category.

   - **Store Category, Secondary:** Give your store front page, secondary keywords, and categories some careful thought. This is how buyers on the Internet will land at your store.

SEE ALSO **Chapter 7, "Find the Best Keywords"**

Note that nearly all eBay Stores are set up wrong. The best information I have found on eBay Store SEO and proper setup is a video series available at www.storessuccessvideo.com/studentrate. It shows you step-by-step how to get your store products on the first page of Google search results.

The Selling Strategy for eBay Stores

I have been asked this question many times: "If a seller has an eBay Store, does he or she still need to create standard listings on eBay?" My answer is absolutely! You must run concurrent regular auctions to draw customers to your eBay Store. Without standard listings, "If you build it, they won't come."

Buyers won't come because they don't know your store exists. For most standard searches on eBay, store items are not included in the search results. Therefore, you need to run standard listings concurrently with eBay Store listings. In your standard listings, you encourage the buyer to visit your eBay Store.

In our methodology, the standard listings we will create on eBay will be called our "bait" products. Therefore, the best eBay Store strategy is to sell your best products on eBay as bait, then within that listing description send your buyers to your store to purchase other items.

Determine Your Bait Products

You really must have bait listings running constantly on eBay in order to draw buyers to your store. You need the leverage of the listings so that your customers can find you. Then, within your listings' descriptions, send them to your eBay Store. Sales leverage is created because a good bait listing can create a multiple-product sale.

Primarily, you want to use bait products to act as the lure that attracts attention and interest in your listings. Having already completed the product analysis phase of our methodology, you can now easily determine your own bait products.

The most popular primary products—those with the highest number of hits, the highest demand, on eBay's Hot List, or that consistently bring the best listing success rate (LSR)—are your bait products. Products that are mostly add-on items, upgrades, or impulse buys are your store products.

Creating Bait Product Listings

You will want maximum exposure on eBay, so list bait products in Auction-Style format for 10 days or Fixed Price for 30 days. Be sure (this is very important) to provide a link (or even better, several links) within your listing to view other similar items in your store. This is very easy to accomplish by inserting **Click Here** links in your description using Turbo Lister or eBay's standard Sell Your Item (SYI) form.

SEE ALSO **Chapter 12, "Creating Click Here Links"**

List items that would be great add-on or impulse buys as your store inventory. Ideal store items would include the accessories for your bait product. For example, if your bait product is a camera, sell a camera bag or memory card upgrade in your store.

Place other items that are related to your bait products in your store. Customers that may begin to lose interest in your bait product listing may be attracted to other items you mention in your description that you have in your store. So mention your other items in your description as well and provide a link.

When you create these links in your description, don't use a general phrase such as "To see all my other great items, go to my store." Buyers would have little interest in clicking because you have not given them a reason to look at the items. Instead, write an advertisement such as, "We also carry product 1, product 2, product 3, and a full line of product 4 in our eBay Store. Save money with our combined shipping discounts. Be sure to check our Bargain Bin! **Click Here** to view these items now."

That is a much better enticement for customers to want to visit your store. Even if they are not interested in those particular products, nearly everyone is interested in looking at a category called Bargain Bin. Place items in your store's Bargain Bin that are not selling well with standard listings. List them at an irresistible price and move them out!

Advanced Store Listing Strategies

As your store selling progresses, you should consider using more advanced strategies. In this section, I have provided more progressive strategies that I have used and found to be the most successful.

Strategy for Selling Men's Items

Most men shop on eBay like they do at the mall. When they find an item of interest, they want to buy it immediately. They don't want to wait to see if they win an auction, then have to try it all again if they don't. Most men tend to make buying decisions quickly. Therefore, try this strategy when selling men's items in your store.

When you have several of the same (and very popular) items to sell, create a store listing for the items and list the quantity. Then use a 10-day Auction-Style bait listing for the same item (at a low starting price, possibly with a reserve if needed) and send buyers to your store to purchase it at Fixed Price. In your auction, write a banner heading at the top of your listing such as the following:

"Don't want to wait for the auction to end? **Click Here** to buy this item now from our eBay Store!"

While they are at your store, they will see other items. Hopefully they will purchase accessories, upgrade their selection, or choose something else.

This strategy is different than just using a Fixed Price listing because your intent of the auction listing is advertisement, not to sell that item necessarily. They click the bait listing and then click through to buy the item or other items from your store. With a Fixed Price format, the listing would end as soon as the item sells. With this strategy, your listing remains on eBay drawing in even more buyers until the auction ends. You could also experiment with a Fixed Price listing and try selling quantities greater than one.

Offer a Volume Discount

Another strategy is to list a single item at auction and then send buyers to your store for a volume discount. Let's say your bait product is one Yankee candle. Using this strategy, instead of selling 1 candle for $8, you can sell 10 candles for $70.

List one of your most popular candles on eBay. Within the bait listing write the following:

> "Save $10 on quantity and $5 on shipping,
> **Click Here** and get 10 from our
> eBay Store now!"

This works. In fact, it is funny. Sometimes my bait item doesn't even sell (no bids for the entire week), but meanwhile I have sold 6 to 10 of the "specials" from my store that week because I used that phrase in my bait listing.

For items that are more valuable, I have tried this same technique using eBay's Featured Plus upgrade. Although this is an expensive listing enhancement, you will gain considerable exposure because your listing will be placed toward the top of the results screen for the entire listing duration. When I have used this strategy, I can receive five to seven times my normal volume of hits for my item when compared to a standard listing.

Cross-Promote Your Products

One of the best benefits of eBay Store ownership is the automatic cross-promotion of your store items with your standard listings. When you create an Auction-Style or Fixed Price listing, other products from the same store category will be displayed in your listing. Many of your customers will find something of interest and click through to view the listing. This is an automated process provided by eBay that allows for upselling and add-on opportunities.

Cross-Promote Your Products

The cross-promoted products are selected randomly by eBay from the same category as the standard listings. However, you can also manually choose which products to display. There are also two different levels of cross-promotion. One set of products is displayed when viewing the listing, and a second set can be shown during checkout.

You should choose related products when a listing is being viewed and accessory products during checkout. For example, if you are selling cameras, show other brand names or models during the listing. Then, once a camera has been purchased, show the camera bag and other camera accessories during checkout.

Use Markdown Manager and Have a Sale

Markdown Manager is an eBay tool used to create special sales, promotions, and campaigns for your store. The tool will place a discounted red sales tag on your product that draws immediate attention to the listing. You can discount products by either a percentage or by a specific dollar amount. Markdown Manager also provides a countdown to when the sale ends, which is beneficial to convert a browser to a buyer.

You can also incorporate your store newsletter tool to create sales campaigns. Use Markdown Manager to schedule when you want the promotion to begin and end. You can then send e-mails to your subscriber list to announce your promotion and track the results in your store traffic reports.

SEE ALSO **Chapter 12, "Store Traffic Reports"**

Send Newsletters to Your Customers

Storeowners can send e-mail newsletters to their customer base. When buyers are viewing a storeowner's listing, there is a link to sign up for his or her newsletter. EBay will manage the e-mail subscription activity.

When you are having a special sale or promotion, be sure to send a newsletter to your subscribers. This is a great feature to promote sales campaigns using Markdown Manager.

Create Your "About the Seller" Store Page

Every eBay storeowner has an "About the Seller" page. You should use this page to make your buyer more confident in dealing with you.

This is not the place for pictures of your family and telling us how much you like to water ski. It is about marketing your business and what your business will do for the buyer. It should be friendly and reassuring. Keep it professional yet light. For example:

- List your store's commitment to customer service.

- List store policies.

- Provide guarantees (100% money-back guarantee for 30 days).

- Describe the types of items you carry.

- Encourage buyers to come back often, as you are always adding new products.

- Encourage them to contact you with any questions.

Look at your top competitors, pick out a few "About the Seller" descriptions that look great, and use those as your guide. Think like Nordstrom and write about your excellent customer service.

Your eBay Store should be known for truthful descriptions, fair prices, quality products, and numerous repeat customers.

eBay Store Referral Credit Program

If you own a website, you can receive a credit off your Final Value Fees by sending traffic to your eBay Store. On your website, you encourage buyers to visit your eBay Store to see your current bargains. You will use a special link that eBay provides you for this purpose. The link informs eBay that this buyer has arrived from your website. If they purchase an item from your store, eBay will refund 75 percent of your Final Value Fee for that item. To learn more, click eBay's **Help** link and type **about the store referral credit.**

10 Drop Shipping

At a recent eBay Live convention, I had the privilege of meeting an eBay Titanium PowerSeller. He averages sales of over $150,000 each and every month on eBay. At the show he was a very busy young man (in his late 20s), but he agreed to stop and speak with me for a few minutes. I had many questions.

I asked him what he sells and he said, "Mostly computers, components, and accessories." He also builds custom-made computers for his customers. I asked him how long he has been selling on eBay and he replied, "About four years." When I asked him how he became such a high-volume seller on eBay in such a short time, he simply said, "Drop shipping ... of course!" He no longer needs to drop ship. He has his own warehouse, and his employees build the custom computers.

His response confirmed how many eBay PowerSellers become high volume sellers so quickly. His eBay business went from first gear into overdrive within just a few months because of drop shipping.

Drop Shipping Means eBay in Overdrive

Drop shippers are wholesalers (usually distributors) that will ship individual items to customers for online sellers, including eBay. Many sellers use drop shipping for business leverage because it allows them to sell high-end products without the financial burden of having to actually stock the items. Instead, they simply list and sell the item on eBay, then contact their drop ship distributor to have the item sent to their customer. The distributor ships the item and charges the wholesale cost, plus shipping, to the eBay seller. The seller collects the profit without having ever touched the product!

Because no inventory is actually stocked, eBay sellers who use drop shippers can sell a lot of products and shift their business from first gear to overdrive almost immediately. Think of the advantages when using drop shippers. Most eBay sellers have at least enough stock on hand for one month of sales. If you have a higher value product that sells for $500, it would cost you about $250 wholesale. If you sold three of these products per week, that is 12 per month. This means you would have to spend $3,000 in inventory per month just to sell that one product. Now compare that to your inventory cost when using a drop shipper—$0.

Do you see the enormous leverage and advantage here? How many products can you afford to sell when your inventory costs nothing? As many as you can list!

Does this sound like a good deal? It is, as long as you do it correctly. There are some cautions with drop shipping that you need to clearly understand.

The Good, the Bad, and the Ugly

There are some disadvantages associated with using drop shippers. First, because you do not physically ship the product, you place your eBay feedback in the drop shipper's hands. You need to be sure the drop shipper is reputable and will provide professional and timely shipping fulfillment for you.

The second problem is that you are not in control of your drop shipper's inventory. What if you list a drop ship item on eBay, and after it sells, you find that your drop shipper is out of stock? Bad feedback will be coming your way.

Did you just get a cold chill? Don't worry. Most problems for eBay sellers are simple to resolve, and this is one of them. The solution for this problem is that you always have enough inventory in your personal stock to cover all of your outstanding listings for that item. If your drop shipper is out of stock, you simply ship your customer the product from your personal inventory. Then you don't list that product again until the drop shipper has restocked.

This does mean that you are going to have to stock some inventory. So to solve the out-of-stock problem, your inventory is not zero, but it is still significantly less than having to stock an entire month's worth of that product. You just need enough to cover your eBay listings. If you sell 3 a week, you need 3 but not 12.

The Drop Shipper Inventory Checklist

To avoid the out-of-stock problem altogether, there is an extra step to your inventory management. You will have to keep track of your own stock as well as the stock of the product from the drop shippers you use. Once again, this also has a simple solution.

You can efficiently track your drop shipper's inventory by using the Drop Shipper Inventory Checklist. It is available as part of the free worksheet downloads from www.trainingu4auctions.com/notebook.

You will complete a Drop Shipper Inventory Checklist at least once a week for each drop shipper that you use. I complete my forms the day of or the day before I list my drop ship items on eBay. If you are relisting the same products each week, then use a new checklist, write the product names and inventory stock numbers in the columns provided, and make several copies. This way you will not have to keep writing the same information for each product each week.

Most of my drop shippers offer online ordering. Therefore, I login to my drop shipper's ordering system and check the inventory for the products I plan to sell. I have already determined their minimum "in stock" quantity that I require before I list the item. You determine this by speaking with a salesperson from the drop shipping company. Ask for a firm number that the company considers to be enough quantity so that it will not run out of stock for at least one week. Usually this number is the same every week unless you sell seasonal items. After a period of time of working with a particular drop shipper, you can adjust the minimum quantity. When you begin, use the number that the salesperson provides. Write that number in the column labeled Minimum Required Inventory Quantity # on your checklist.

The day before you list your item, login to your supplier's site to check its stock for each product it drop ships for you. Write the actual inventory quantity in the column Actual Inventory Quantity #.

Now compare the two columns, Minimum Required and Actual Inventory. This checklist is an "exception" list, meaning that if there is sufficient inventory you make no mark on the sheet. If, however, you find a product that is low on inventory, it is an exception. Therefore, place a check mark in the Do Not List column for that item.

Drop Shipper Inventory Checklist

Complete a worksheet each week for every drop shipper you use.

Drop Shipper: _____

In-Stock Inventory Quantities for Week of: _____

Product Name	Product Inventory Stock #	Minimum Required Inventory Quantity #	Actual Inventory Quantity #	Do Not List! ✓

Note to Printer: This page is not copyrighted. The reader can make as many copies of this page as they require. Kevin W. Boyd

Drop Shipper Inventory Checklist

You now have an inventory checklist for each drop shipper you use. When you create your eBay listings the next day, you can quickly scan the list to see which products you should not list that week. All of your other products can be listed without concern. Again, a simple solution.

Yes, this is a bit of effort, but this is your business. The effort required is minor, and the problems you will avoid are major if by chance your drop shipper is out of stock for a product you just sold. If you combine both safety nets—the drop shipper checklist along with stocking your own inventory—then it is highly unlikely you will run out of stock.

Are You Ready for Drop Shipping?

I use and recommend drop shippers for eBay sellers. Before you proceed with this method of order fulfillment, however, make sure you are ready.

- You should be an experienced eBay seller. It is best that you have at least 50 to 100 successfully completed sales transactions and possibly already be a PowerSeller before you undertake this.

- Drop shipping is not for the occasional seller. You must stay current with your drop shipper's inventory. Will you conduct this important step before you list your items each week?

- Can you afford to have at least one of each product in your own stock in case of a back order?

- Often you will need to call, e-mail, or place an order with your drop shipper during the day. Can you do that from work?

These are some of the factors to consider if you are just starting to sell on eBay. If you believe you are ready and are determined to advance, drop shipping is one of the quickest ways to get a successful eBay business up and running.

If you decide to use drop shippers, remember that your feedback is in their hands. So, while I do recommend drop shipping as powerful selling leverage for your eBay business, I suggest you do it correctly.

The first step is to ensure that you are dealing with reputable drop shippers. Second, since you need backup inventory anyway, you should test the quality, professionalism, and timeliness of their fulfillment services by having a few products shipped to you. This way, you will experience their entire process before using them to serve your customers.

The most important step is to find and work with only reputable drop shippers. Obviously, the word "reputable" is mentioned often with regard to product suppliers. I cannot stress this enough. It is imperative to locate and use companies known for quality products, fair business dealings, and sterling customer service. So, how do you find them quickly and easily?

How to Find Reputable Drop Shippers

I personally use and recommend Worldwide Brands (WWB) to find drop shippers. It is the only drop ship directory publisher that is certified by eBay. It has also made my eBay business so much easier with all of its product sourcing databases and online seller tools such as Instant Market Research.

Worldwide Brands's Databases

You were introduced to Worldwide Brands's package of database products and Internet seller research tools in Chapter 3. We used WWB's Instant Market Research tool again as part of your product research methodology in Chapter 5. In Chapter 6, I explained how to use the company to find reputable wholesalers, especially drop shippers. By now you understand why Worldwide Brands is viewed so favorably by eBay PowerSellers.

As a member of the Worldwide Brands site (Product Sourcing Membership), you simply enter the brand name or type of product you are looking for, and the site will find a drop shipper or other type of wholesaler for you that has been preapproved by Worldwide Brands's stringent approval process. The site also provides excellent training (The Whole$ale eBiz Education program) to help you learn the details about drop shipping, as well as eBay or Internet product sourcing.

There are a lot of quacks and outright scammers on the Internet that claim to be drop shippers. Don't try to find one on your own. Remember that the only drop ship directory provider that is certified by eBay is www.worldwidebrands.com/studentrate.

Working with Drop Shippers

Once you have located your drop shippers, you need to contact them to request a dealer application.

SEE ALSO **Chapter 6, "Complete the Dealer Application"**

When you are approved and are assigned a salesperson, phone the person to review the ordering and fulfillment processes. You want to be sure that you ask the following questions:

- What shipping carrier do they use?
- Will they ship internationally for you? What about shipping to APO/FPO military addresses?
- What will the shipping label and invoice have as the return address—you or the drop shipper?
- How soon will they ship after an order is placed?
- How do they notify you of shipments?

- How do they handle and notify you about backorders?

- How do you pay for your products?

- How will they handle product returns from you or your customer?

Also determine the minimum inventory quantities for every product they will drop ship for you. Use these numbers in your Drop Shipper Inventory Checklist.

Selling Drop Ship Products

You will need a picture of the drop shipped product when you create your listing. Many eBay sellers use the manufacturer's photo. You learned in Chapter 7, however, that you need to take your own photo. Otherwise your listing will look like all the others. Be the contrarian and take your own professional-looking photos. Now you are the one that is different, and this will attract the desired attention.

When creating the shipping portion of your listing, use the same carrier and type of services that your drop shipper will use. Choose the calculated rate for UPS or USPS shipments or use a flat rate from your drop shipper's fulfillment center location. Be sure to add all extra costs such as insurance.

You should sell drop shipped items at Fixed Price or, at the very least, Auction-Style with a reserve. You cannot afford to sell these items at auction with a low starting price. You are going to pay full wholesale when you order the product, so you need to be sure that you will receive your desired profit margin.

SEE ALSO **Chapter 5, "Minimum Profit Margin"**

Ordering Your Drop Shipped Products

Once your product sells, wait for the notification of payment e-mail from PayPal before you begin the fulfillment process. After you receive confirmation of the buyer's payment, contact your drop ship salesperson or use the company's online ordering system to place your order. You need to decide whether to add insurance for the package.

Most wholesalers ship by UPS, so that includes $100 worth of coverage for the contents. If the item is worth more than this, I suggest you add the additional insurance.

As soon as you order, expect that the drop shipper will charge your credit card that's on file from your dealer application. You will receive a receipt through the mail or by e-mail. Keep these receipts in an organized file for your tax records.

When the package is shipped, you will most likely be notified by e-mail from the drop shipper. If tracking information is included, it is good customer service to send a brief e-mail to your customer. Include the tracking number and carrier's website. The e-mail should serve to replace the "thank you" letter that you would have placed in the box. Thank the buyer for his or her purchase and provide instructions for how to contact you if necessary.

Now you see the advantages of selling your eBay items with the help of a drop shipper. At first you may think you are a salesperson for them. I would like you to view it in reverse. The drop shipper is your fulfillment center.

With drop shipping, you will be spending less time receiving, storing, packing, and shipping products. You can also quickly expand your business, selling multiple products with inventory that you do not have to shelve or even purchase until sold.

Expand Your eBay Business

During the "reality check" discussion in Chapter 1, you learned the number one mistake new eBay sellers make is that they usually make their product selection decisions based on one primary reason—the items are cheap!

These sellers have no method to their product selection decisions. They just buy products used for resale on eBay based on hunches and guesswork. "Hey, here's an item that is really cheap. I'll bet I could make some money with this thing!" The operative word here is "bet." Their listings are a roll of the dice.

With what you now know about the need for formal product selection methodology, doesn't this mistake seem senseless? It can be so easily avoided. Yet eBay sellers continue making this same mistake over and over again.

In my opinion, the biggest difference between eBay amateurs and professionals is exactly what you have learned in this book. The amateur makes product decisions based on whims and impulse buys with hit-or-miss results. Professionals use a solid methodology to ensure that the items they are about to purchase for resale are already proven profitable on eBay before they even place their product order.

There is also a primary difference between somewhat successful eBay sellers and those who have built a thriving eBay business. It is how they expand and grow their business.

Develop a Thriving eBay Business

Most successful eBay sellers tend to stay within their comfort zone. Many have found a niche and have sold successfully there for months or years. When they decide they want to increase their eBay revenue, they stick with what they know. They attempt growth by selling more and more related products that are all still within their niche.

Expansion within your niche is fine as long as every item is profitable. Many times, however, this is not the case, and it results in diminishing returns. The problem with expansion in only one niche is that, as you have seen, when you expand your niche's product line beyond its demand, you begin to see the red-priced, no-sale listings on eBay. So when sellers try to expand within their niche, they often create more work, increase their costs with listing fees and inventory stock, but do not increase their sales revenue because the items are not selling. In an attempt to take one step forward, they actually take two steps back.

EBay professionals who manage a thriving business will stick with their product selection methodology and only add items to their product line that are proven profitable. Once the profitable product line is exhausted for their niche, these sellers don't try to expand by adding unprofitable items. Instead, they add other niches.

Simply stated, to develop a thriving eBay business, don't stop at your first niche. Cherry pick your items from the top sellers of niche #1. Then repeat that process in niche #2, niche #3, niche #4, and so on until you build the income-producing business you desire.

I like to think of all these niches as mini businesses. I actually refer to them as the "divisions" that are within my overall eBay business. In each division, I am selling small quantities of profitable items that are completely unrelated to the other divisions. I may even use a different type of product sourcing and selling method for each division.

You should plan to create divisions within your eBay business as well. The following are a few examples:

Division 1, General Sales: This could be general sales of several unrelated items. Your products will most likely be purchased from surplus stores and liquidators. You will use Auction-Style and Fixed Price listings for the most part. If this division becomes large, open a general sales eBay Store.

Division 2, Specialty Sales: Open a specialty item "niche" eBay Store. Run concurrent Auction-Style and Fixed Price listings that draw buyers to your store. Your products will most likely be purchased from large-volume or light-bulk wholesalers.

Division 3, Drop Ship: Drop ship higher-priced items that are either specialty products in an eBay Store or Auction-Style listings. Purchase your items from drop ship wholesalers.

To build a solid eBay business, then, you should create several mini divisions and sell only the most profitable products in those categories and niches. Each division will sell different, unrelated items. Collectively, however, they contribute to your total sales and profit.

Building a solid eBay business is a simple numbers game. For example, if your first division has 20 products that you sell on average for a $15 profit and you sell each product at least once a week, division #1 is producing $1,200 in monthly profits. If you desire $6,000 a month from eBay income, you will need at least five divisions with similar results. Success is just that simple now that you know the methodology.

Therefore, after you have used these methods to produce your first profitable division, start the research all over again looking for products to start a new division. If needed, open another eBay User ID (account) and another eBay Store to sell your new products. Then add more and more divisions, niches, stores, and products until you have built the business you desire.

Expand by Selling Internationally

Once you have established your product line(s), you should determine which products might also have global appeal. Then, when you create the listings for these items, be sure to encourage international buyers to buy from you.

The benefit of encouraging international bidders is twofold. First, more than half of all eBay's sales are from international buyers. If you do not allow them to bid on your item, you are closing off half of the potential marketplace. Second, it is most likely that you will still sell the item to a customer in the United States. Allowing international customers to bid on your item, however, will help to raise the final price.

Setting Your Preferences for International Buyers

Creating a listing for international buyers is a two-step process. You must first set your buyer preferences in your My eBay page to only allow bids from buyers in the countries you want to ship to. Second, when you create your listing, you indicate the countries where you agree to ship. Use the following steps to set your international buyer preferences correctly.

Step 1. Set Your Buyer Preferences

To set your buyer preferences, complete the following steps:

1. Select your **My eBay** tab.

2. Under the **My Account** link on the left sidebar, select **Site Preferences.**

3. Under **Selling Preferences,** choose **Buyer Requirements,** and then select **Show.**

4. Select **Edit** under **Block buyers who.**

5. Place a check mark next to **Block buyers who are registered in countries to which I don't ship.**

6. Click **Submit.**

Step 2. Choose Your Countries

Your next step when creating your listings is to select the United States and then add any other countries where you wish to ship. If an international buyer lives in a country that you have not indicated as your shipping preference, eBay will block that customer from bidding on your item. This is a good way to eliminate fraud from countries that are known for buyer scams (you can make an exception on a case-by-case basis if you need to).

During listing creation using the Sell Your Item form, go to the **Maximize your item's visibility** section. If you are using Turbo Lister, the section is called **Listing Upgrades.** Now select the countries where you want your listings to appear in search results. Note that if your particular listing form does not show this section, your product category does not qualify for this feature.

Communication

If international customers have questions, they can communicate with you by sending an e-mail. Most global buyers who are bidding on an item on eBay.com (eBay's U.S. website) understand at least some English. When you receive a question from them, keep your e-mail responses short and to the point. Long answers may confuse non-English-speaking customers.

Receiving Payments

When creating your listings, you should insist that all payments from international buyers be made in U.S. funds and paid for with PayPal. Money orders, cashier's checks, personal checks, and any other method can all be a form of fraud, so don't take the risk and go outside of eBay's required payment system. Since PayPal is now in over 190 countries, there is no reason to accept any other form of payment.

When your international customers receive your invoices from eBay, they can pay for the items using PayPal. They will almost always pay in U.S. funds. If they decide to pay for the items in another currency that is still the equivalent to the U.S. amount, PayPal will send you an e-mail asking for approval. You can decide to accept a different currency or insist on U.S. funds. PayPal charges 2.9 to 3.9 percent plus 30 cents to run a transaction for you that requires conversion from another currency.

Which Shipping Carrier to Use

The only carrier worth considering for shipping individual packages globally is the United States Postal Service. The differences in cost between the USPS and all other carriers is significant.

For my *eBay Business at Your Fingertips* book, I conducted a study comparing the cost of sending a 4-pound package from the United States to several different countries. The USPS averaged about $35 to many countries, but FedEx, UPS, and DHL were about $100. The price differences are so large that I don't even consider it anymore. All my global-bound packages are sent by the USPS.

You can also use Priority Mail boxes (including Flat Rate boxes) for international shipments (called Priority Mail International), as long as the item can fit in the box and weighs less than 20 pounds. You can also print postage and customs forms from your home office and schedule a free carrier pickup for international packages. So unless you are shipping freight, use the USPS for all your international shipments.

If you routinely ship packages to APO/FPO addresses (U.S. military overseas), the USPS provides a 12×12×5½ inch Priority Mail Flat Rate box. The rate is also $2 less than if using the standard Flat Rate boxes. Learn more at www.usps.com.

Determine Your Shipping Rate

You can create eBay listings that include both domestic and international shipping rates. You can even choose a flat rate or a calculated international rate the same way you do for domestic shipments.

To estimate a flat rate using the USPS, go to www.usps.com and choose the **Calculate Postage,** then the **Calculate International Postage** link (You can also calculate postage when completing the Sell Your Item form). You then choose the country, package type, dimensions, and weight. Choose the countries that you will choose to sell to, such as Canada, the UK, European countries, Australia, and so on, to determine their rates.

Then list each country alongside its rates in alphabetical order when writing your description. This will inform your international customers of your rates and will also eliminate several e-mails asking what the shipping rate will be to each country.

Alternatively, you can also use eBay's Calculated Rate option when creating your listing. You will need to provide the shipping carrier, type of service, box dimensions, and weight. EBay will then automatically provide a calculated rate to every international buyer based on the country where he or she lives, as long as the buyer is logged in to his or her eBay account when viewing your item.

Printing Postage and Customs Forms

You can print prepaid postage and even the required Customs Declaration Forms from your home computer, the same way as described for domestic shipments in Chapter 8. The Customs Declaration Form number can also be used as your tracking number to some countries. If you intend to complete these forms yourself, they are available at your local post office.

Customs officers in your buyer's country will use the forms to determine the package contents and then assess the duty (tax). An officer has the right to open the box to confirm the contents you have written on the declaration form.

As the seller, you are responsible to accurately complete the Customs Declaration Form. You will not charge or collect any duty, as this is the function of the customs officer. Use Customs Declaration Forms 2976 or 2976-A for each international package. Form 2976 is the short form and can be used with the free Priority Mail boxes. If you use a different box or are sending the package Express Mail International, use form 2976-A.

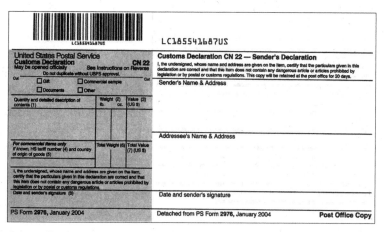

Customs Form 2976

These are very simple forms to complete. You provide your name and address, your customer's name and address, and a very brief description of the package's contents and value.

Customs Form 2976-A

Expand Your Customer Base with Marketing

You can promote your business by using techniques other than standard listings and an eBay Store. EBay provides several ways and tools to advertise your business. Explore ways to promote and market your business outside of eBay. Greater exposure creates interest in you, your business, and your products, which leads to more store visits and sales.

My World and About the Seller Pages

You should create both a My World page and an About the Seller (or About Me) page for your User ID. Use these pages to discuss your business specialties, your commitment to customer service, and the benefits of purchasing items from you. There is no charge for either type of page.

Every seller has a My World page. It is up to you whether you want to customize it. You will need to create an About the Seller page. Sellers who have opened an About the Seller page have a "me" logo next to their User ID.

SEE ALSO **Chapter 9, "Create Your 'About the Seller' Store Page"**

Discussion Boards

EBay provides Discussion Boards, which are forums for members with similar interests to connect and communicate. There are currently over 95 different and active Discussion Boards on eBay.

The Community Help, Category-Specific, and General Discussion Boards are the most active boards. You can visit them, join a discussion, and provide useful insights to other's questions and problems that are related to the products you sell.

You should not outright advertise your products on these boards, but you can certainly use a signature line that includes your eBay User ID and a link to your eBay Store. You may be viewed as an expert or possibly create interest in you or your products. Many readers will want to see your product listings.

Include Advertising Flyers in Your Packages

Just before you seal your packages, place a promotional flyer or a "thank you" letter on top. This will be the first thing your customers see when they open their packages.

Offer discounts, give freebies, and provide reasons for them to come back to your eBay Store. In your letter, encourage them to sign up for your newsletter so you can inform them of special promotions and sales. Ask them to tell their friends. At a minimum, encourage them to leave positive feedback for you.

EBay storeowners have access to templates that can help you easily create and print flyers. If you don't have a store, you can create flyers yourself using Microsoft Word or an art-centric application. Make a copy of your flyer and take it to a copy center for reproduction. Choose a colorful, eye-catching paper stock such as yellow, pink, or blue with black text.

Create Newsletters

It is always easier to get additional sales from a satisfied customer than it is to convince a new customer to purchase from you. A great way to do this on eBay is to use newsletters to market to your current customer base. If you have an eBay Store, eBay provides the tools to create outstanding newsletter campaigns.

SEE ALSO **Chapter 9, "Send Newsletters to Your Customers"**

Attend Trade Shows

Attend trade shows that are related to the categories on eBay where you sell or are interested in selling. Network with the booth vendors to see if there is synergy between their products or services and your business goals.

Before you attend, get a logo and print numerous business cards. Hand your cards out to any prospective supplier or customer. Make appointments with key suppliers and individuals either during or after the show. The first time you attend, you are there mainly as a buyer to learn and make supplier contacts. The next year you may be there as a vendor yourself.

SEE ALSO **Appendix D, "Other Helpful Sites and Products"**

You can find most major trade shows in the United States from the www.tsnn.com website. Also check trade magazines, subscribe to newsletters, and conduct Internet searches using keywords such as "trade show" and "conference."

Open a Blog

Did you know that you can open a blog (web log) on eBay for free? This is an excellent way to market your eBay business on the Internet!

You would first create an informative, newsletter style of blog and then optimize it so that search engines can find you quickly. In your blog, you can discuss your business and products. You can also promote your blog in your About the Seller (for sellers with a store or About Me page for sellers with no store) and My World pages. To learn more about opening an eBay blog, use the link http://blogs.ebay.com/ebaynii@ebay.com.

SEE ALSO **Chapter 9, "Create Your 'About the Seller' Store Page"**

Improve Your Customer Base

Selling on eBay can be time-consuming. Tracking down deadbeats is very frustrating and wastes a lot of time. From personal experience, I have learned how to improve a customer base and avoid the most risky customers and their associated problems.

I have considerable experience selling several items in different categories and price ranges. Through this experience, I discovered where most of my problem buyers and deadbeats were coming from and eventually determined how best to avoid them. Once I changed the items I was selling, the auction formats, and price ranges accordingly, I improved my customer base and minimized my problems. I suggest you do the same and avoid potential risk.

First, let's examine the following customer base chart. I have compared the associated risk from different customer groups. Risk is defined as either deadbeats who don't pay for items they have won or those who may leave undeserved poor or negative feedback.

Note that the information in this chart (and the advice in this chapter) is based entirely on my experiences selling on eBay. I have no statistics for my conclusions. I am merely explaining where I have found problem customers and how I now try to avoid them.

eBay Customer Base to Risk* Comparison			
Customer Base	Item Price	Auction Risk*	Fixed Price Risk*
Group 1	$.01–$20	High	Medium to High
Group 2	$20–$50	Medium	Low
Group 3	$50–$100	Low	Low
Group 4	$100–$300	Low	Low
Group 5	$300–$1,000	Medium	Low to Medium
Group 6	$1,000+	Medium to High	Low to Medium

Risk is defined as either UPIs (unpaid item deadbeats) or negative feedback.

A few immediate observations can be drawn from this chart:

- Your risk is highest when you sell items that are under $20 using the Auction-Style format.

- If you sell items under $20, you can lower your risk by selling them using the Fixed Price format.

- All Fixed Price listings are low risk when compared to auctions.

- Fixed Price listings selling between $20 and $300 and Auction-Style listings between $50 and $300 offer the lowest risk.

- Selling to high-end customers (over $1,000) may also increase risk.

Customer Base Conclusions and Recommendations

Avoid selling items that are under $20 (group 1) and especially under $10. I have found that the most whiners, complainers, unpaid items, and negative feedback threats come from buyers of items that actually sold for under $10. They aren't looking for a deal, they are looking for a steal. Antique shop and used bookstore owners who were students in my classes told me they experience the same problem.

I can sell items for $200 and encounter few problem buyers. However, it seems that as soon as I sell some item for $5, I'll get an e-mail threat of negative feedback if the item isn't there in three days, or I never hear from them again. Amazing but true many times.

This is because these types of bidders place multiple bids on many items. They are not necessarily serious about wanting your item over all the others. Sometimes when they win your item, they may choose to just not pay and ignore your payment reminder e-mails.

You can eliminate some of this risk by selling items under $20 at Fixed Price. Buyers usually don't click on a Fixed Price, "Buy It Now" button unless they intend to pay for it. You can also require immediate PayPal payment during listing creation. This means that your listing doesn't end until the winning bidder has paid for the item.

Also, watch your shipping and handling rates on items that are under $20. Handling charges are the basis for many complaints and low Detailed Seller Ratings (DSRs). People who are shopping in these categories are looking for a bargain on everything. They scrutinize everything and may complain about your shipping or handling price in their feedback comments about you.

You are not making much money selling items under $20 anyway. It takes just as long to list, pack, and ship a $5 item as it does a $50 item. Sell items to customers in groups 2, 3, and 4, and you will make more money and avoid a lot of this risk. You can also sell in groups 5 and 6, but your risk requires consideration.

Avoiding Other Deadbeats

The age of the buyer can also have an effect on your deadbeat ratio. Based on my experience, I can say this simply: avoid selling items that would especially appeal to teenagers and college students.

These are winning bidders who often run and hide. Maybe they didn't intend to win the item. They were just sitting around the dorm with their friends and, oops, they won your iPod auction. "But I don't have the money. I don't know what to do. Let's just not respond and maybe the seller will leave us alone." Now you are stuck tracking them down and eventually filing an Unpaid Item (UPI) form just to get your eBay fees back.

I am not saying you shouldn't sell video games and "head banging" music that you just want to get rid of. What I am saying is not to make items that appeal to teenagers part of your eBay business product line. Teenagers do not have much money and can be fickle when it comes to payment responsibility and business acumen.

Selling items that appeal to teenagers and college students may be a sound business decision if you sell video games at a mall or from your own website but not on eBay. If you are still not convinced, ask yourself this question, "Do you really want to place your excellent feedback score in the hands of some teenagers who may be irresponsible?"

Understandably, there are always exceptions. I have been the mentor to several high school students who sold items on eBay as their senior projects. I was encouraged by their diligence, thoroughness, and organization to complete the projects using the methodology taught in my course. I use them as shining examples of responsibility and focus. It was also interesting that they all agreed they would not want some of their own friends as eBay customers.

Manage Your eBay Business

Throughout this book, you have learned how to find and sell profitable products on eBay. There is, however, another important component to your eBay business—the management of resources and costs. Carefully monitoring and controlling costs will keep your business afloat during the rough periods and will allow for expansion during the boom times. In this chapter, we will discuss the management of inventory, fixed and variable costs, and software tools to help manage your eBay business.

The eBay Product Life Cycle

As mentioned in Chapter 4, every product sold on eBay has a life cycle. A successful product will have a span that includes the phases of introduction, growth, maturity, and decline. The amount of sales and length of time for each phase is different for every product. This makes the growth and continuation of each phase difficult to predict. Tracking the sales history of your products will help to identify the decline. You need to be careful because you don't want to be stuck with inventory that has no further life on eBay.

Monitor Your Product's Life Cycle

If you sell products that are in the declining phase, you need to track your month-to-month sales. As long as sales (both price and volume) for these items remain constant, you can continue to carry them. Eventually you will notice that one of your products had lower-than-normal sales for a particular month. That is a red flag warning, and you need to investigate.

It could be that you are selling seasonal items. As you progress through the seasons, items such as clothing and sporting goods will have peaks and valleys instead of a steady demand and sales stream. This is one reason eBay has modified the PowerSeller program to enable seasonal sellers to qualify.

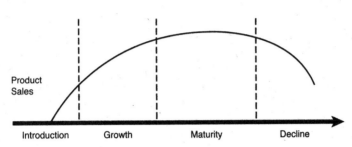

The Product Life Cycle

The Product Life Cycle

Another problem could be that new competition has arrived suddenly. Maybe an inexperienced eBay seller has decided to sell the same product and is listing the item for little or no profit. The person is selling the items for substantially less than you are, and all the buyers are going to those listings. It could also be that a competitor has decided to stop selling this product and is dumping it on eBay using auctions that have a very low starting price.

When you find a sudden decline in sales, you need to investigate and determine what is causing it. If you cannot find a reason such as those just mentioned, you have to consider the possibility that demand for your product has decreased, and it is on the declining phase of its life cycle.

Pull Your Weeds

If you have a product that is no longer bringing the sales or profit that you desire, you can use analysis tools such as HammerTap to track and study the product's sales history and check for new competitors. Use Worldwide Brands's Instant Market Research tools as well to determine the total online demand for the product.

If you have decided that the eBay marketplace has moved on from that product, it is time for you to move on as well. Think of it much like the stock market. When professional speculators see that their "moving averages" are slipping, they pull the trigger and dump the stock. You want to move quickly as well before the demand for your product drops to the point of unprofitability. Have a fire sale and move those products out.

If for any reason you guessed wrong and the product comes back strong, you can always reenter the marketplace later and sell it again. The risk is not in selling off too soon but in holding inventory for a product that is on a steep and rapid decline.

Managing Your Inventory

I am going to make the assumption that you have limited discretionary funds for your eBay business. Therefore, you will need to budget wisely for business supplies and product inventory.

Just like other retail businesses, eBay sellers have many expenses. Most of your allotted budgetary funds will be used for your biggest expense—inventory. Many eBay sellers, however, often make the mistake of spending too much money on unnecessarily large amounts of inventory.

In the 1980s and with the progress of the computer age, a new concept entered the world of manufacturing. It was called just-in-time manufacturing. It was a concept that revolutionized manufacturing and assembly lines in the 1980s and is still in use today.

The concept is that large assembly-line manufacturers (such as Boeing or General Motors) stock short-term inventory. The parts from their crosstown suppliers are unloaded from the trucks at the loading docks and then placed in a temporary staging area for a few hours or days, then are maneuvered again to the required location on the assembly line "just in time" for assembly.

The inventory cost savings is enormous for large companies that use this process. Now their biggest problem is what to do with all that empty warehouse space that is no longer needed.

I use the just-in-time concept for inventory management of my eBay business. I do not keep large quantities of inventory for any particular item. Instead, I watch my inventory stock closely. I understand very thoroughly the average quantity of each item I sell each week as well as the lead-time required from each of my suppliers. As soon as my inventory is getting low, I place an order with my supplier in just enough time to resupply my stock before it sells out. So while my sold eBay items are moving out the front door with the USPS, my inventory resupply is coming in the back door from UPS and FedEx.

I usually can turn over my entire inventory once and sometimes even twice a month. In short, the money I save by keeping my inventory low and moving product quickly is now free to be used for other business purposes such as purchasing different items to sell.

The only exception to this rule is during the holiday selling season (September through December). You need to stock considerable inventory because sometimes even suppliers run out of stock during this time.

For maximum profit, then, you need to carry many different items that turn over quickly. Use just-in-time inventory management so you can benefit from "broad and thin" inventory, not "narrow and deep." This is the wisest use of your inventory money. It allows for a larger product line in which each product generates a profit for you rather than a narrow and deep product line that is mostly taking up space in your garage and will take much longer to sell.

eBay Markets Shift and Change

Another reason not to go deep in inventory is that the eBay marketplace is fluid and moves at a rapid pace. Fads and trends come and go. What was hot or fashionable even six months ago may not be hot now. Maybe customers for your products have now moved on to the latest fashions or newer models.

Consider the unfortunate seller who went deep in inventory with the first generation of iPods and then the second model was introduced. Immediately, his items sold for less than what he paid for them. If you are selling mass-market, high-tech items, do not go deep into inventory because the introduction of a new model can destroy your profits overnight. Why do you think companies liquidate items?

If you sell the same items on eBay relisting them repeatedly every week, be careful to watch your monthly sales. Over time, your products may become saturated and stale with little or no demand. When you notice a definite downturn in sales, consider lowering the price and encouraging your repeat customers to buy now before the inventory is depleted. In your e-mailed newsletter, describe an upcoming item you will be selling. Create interest for the future while eliminating any leftover older stock.

SEE ALSO **Chapter 9, "Send Newsletters to Your Customers"**

Managing Costs

A large bite out of your profit comes from your inventory costs. The cost for the products you sell (cost of goods sold, or COGS) should be recorded and tracked either in an accounting system such as Quick-Books or an Excel spreadsheet, or at a minimum you should keep sales receipts in a file folder.

There are other costs for your business that you must track as well. These include fixed costs such as overhead for office space and variable costs such as eBay and PayPal fees.

When I hear eBay sellers complain about their seller fees, I ask them how much they think it costs to rent retail space in a mall. You can complain, take your business elsewhere, or just accept the fact that you must pay the fees. The way to view it is that the fees eBay charges are a part of your cost of doing business.

There are three types of fees on eBay:

- Insertion Fee
- Final Value Fee
- Listing Upgrade Fee

Each is slightly different and can affect your profit for each item you sell, so it is worth understanding the different fees involved in a listing. You can get a quick calculation estimate for any listing by going to www.ebcalc.com. For a detailed explanation of fees, click on eBay's **Help** link and type **ebay.com fees** in the search box.

Insertion Fee. This is the first charge for listing an item on eBay. The fee is based on the starting price that you choose.

Final Value Fee. A Final Value Fee is also assessed if your item does indeed sell. The fee is also a rolling scale that decreases as the value of your item's price increases.

Listing Upgrade Fees. You can choose to add an upgrade to your listing such as including more pictures or choosing to add a subtitle ($.50), bold ($1), highlight ($5), or a border ($3) around your listing in the search results. These and other upgrades are beyond the standard listing features and come with associated fees. To find the current upgrade fees, go to ebay.com, type **ebay.com fees,** and then choose **Listing Upgrade Fees.**

Don't add enhancements to your listings unless you are sure they will bring more money for the item. (Use HammerTap to determine this.) All of these fees can add up quickly and are applied directly to the cost of selling your item.

PayPal Fees

PayPal charges a fee for each transaction. The fees range from 1.9 to 2.9 percent plus 30 cents per transaction. International transactions that require currency conversions are 2.9 to 3.9 percent plus 30 cents. The currency conversion is also 2.5 percent above the wholesale exchange rate. The actual fee rates you will be charged are based on the monthly sales volume you produce. When you are starting your eBay business, assume the higher range.

Fixed and Variable Costs and Taxes

For tax purposes, you will need to keep track of all your fixed costs. If you rent space, you will have monthly leasing receipts. If you work out of your home, you need to pay yourself rent.

Rent is determined by the amount of space you require for your eBay business as a percentage of your overall living space. If that equals 15 percent, then you should pay yourself 15 percent of the mortgage or rent. You should also include other costs such as phone, Internet, and utility bills.

The largest variable cost would be your product inventory (COGS). Other variable costs would be your supplies, eBay and PayPal fees, shipping and postage fees, and car mileage for any business-related trips. If you travel to trade shows, all travel costs such as airline tickets, hotels, and meals are tax deductible.

I strongly suggest that you not attempt to do your own taxes when you are running a business. You wouldn't think of doing your own dental work. Have a CPA handle your accounting needs and taxes as well. I have found that the amount of money CPAs have saved me more than pays for their services, and their fee is tax deductible on the following year's taxes.

eBay's Accounting Assistant

EBay now makes your record keeping much easier. The entire transaction history of your eBay sales, including the sales details and all eBay and PayPal fees, is ready for electronic download. You can download your history either to an Excel spreadsheet or to QuickBooks and QuickBooks Pro.

If you or your CPA uses QuickBooks, you should use eBay's Accounting Assistant. This program provides a "wizard" that you use to set up the download. Then all records for every transaction are downloaded and inserted directly into your QuickBooks program.

To qualify for this service, you must have the QuickBooks program. You also need to have a subscription to at least one of these eBay software tools:

- eBay Stores
- Selling Manager (sales listing and management tool using My eBay)
- Selling Manager Pro (adds inventory management and automation abilities such as automatic feedback)
- Blackthorne (an offline bulk listing tool)
- Blackthorne Pro (adds inventory management and custom reports)

Get Your Business License

You do not need a business license to sell on eBay, and many sellers choose not to get one. However, you cannot fully utilize the methodology and opportunities presented in this book without one.

The primary reason you should obtain a business license is so you can use wholesalers and drop shippers as suppliers. When you apply for a dealer license with them, one of the first questions on the application will be what your tax ID number is. If you do not have a tax number, they will not sell to you, and your new eBay venture will be stalled. Without a business license, you severely limit your product opportunities. With a license, you have access to every opportunity that you find when using your product selection methodology.

A business license is now easy and inexpensive to obtain if you know where, what, and how to file all the required forms. Best of all, you no longer need to pay expensive attorney fees.

Determine what type of business and licensing pertains to your situation. The most common choices are sole proprietorship, partnership, or the increasingly popular limited liability company (LLC). Most eBay sellers today are choosing the LLC.

The decision as to which type of business is right for you is based mostly on minimizing your taxes. Sole proprietorships are usually taxed about 15 percent higher than LLCs. Plus, an LLC business provides you with security (separating your business liabilities from your personal assets), minimizes paperwork compared with an S or C corporation, and the profits transfer directly to your personal income for much easier tax preparation.

I suggest you speak with your CPA first to determine the best license to obtain. In most cases, the CPA will recommend an LLC. If you would like to speak to an attorney, you can find one free of charge at www.score.org. Score is staffed by retired and experienced attorneys, CPAs, and businesspeople. The company offers advice free of charge to new business owners.

Once you have determined the type of business license you want, you then need to file the paperwork. This is where the high-priced meter starts running when you use an attorney. I suggest you avoid that unnecessary cost.

You can file all the required paperwork by visiting the Business License Division of your state's Department of Licensing. You can accomplish this in person or online. There will be a state fee for your license.

If you don't feel comfortable filing the paperwork yourself, you can get professional help and still not pay expensive attorney fees. Incorporation service providers (ISPs) are online providers of business license services. These sites are designed by attorneys, and the ISP serves as your agent throughout the process. You simply answer about 15 questions online, and the ISP will file all the required paperwork with your state to receive your license.

The benefit of using an ISP is twofold. First, you are getting professional help so you don't miss any important steps in obtaining all the required certificates and licensing. Second, the price charged can be about 85 percent less than what an attorney may charge.

Two of the more popular online incorporation service providers are BizFilings and LegalZoom. You may have heard their advertisements on the radio. If you want professional help with filing an LLC and want to save a lot of money, check out their rates at www.legalzoom.com/studentrate and www.bizfilings.com/studentrate.

Software Tools for Your eBay Business

So far, we have discussed the recommended software tools that will help you find and analyze your products. There are also other tools available to eBay sellers that will help you manage your business. Some are listing tools, and others are complete business management software systems. All are specifically designed to help eBay sellers manage their business.

Turbo Lister

If you are still doing all your listings online to eBay with the Sell Your Item (SYI) form, I suggest you upgrade to Turbo Lister. This listing tool can help you create professional-looking listings much faster and more efficiently. Turbo Lister was developed and is supported by eBay and is available for download free of charge at http://pages.ebay.com/turbo_lister.

With Turbo Lister, instead of having to be connected to eBay when you create your listings, you actually work offline at high speed to your hard drive. This is especially important if you have a slow dial-up connection. Once your listings are complete, you can choose when to send them to eBay. Many sellers who live in areas without high-speed Internet use Turbo Lister to create their listings on their wireless laptop computer, and then they visit a local library or café with wireless service twice a week to upload their listings.

Turbo Lister serves as a database that stores all of your listings. This is an advantage over using eBay's Sell Your Item (SYI) form because eBay removes your listings from its databases after 90 days. With Turbo Lister, all your listings are on your computer's hard drive, so you are in charge of when or if they are removed.

In my opinion, the biggest benefit of Turbo Lister is the ease of duplicating and editing an existing listing to quickly create a new listing. I use this feature often when I sell similar items. I simply create my first listing, duplicate it, edit it to make the required changes, and save it as a new listing.

It is very easy to upload your listings to eBay using Turbo Lister. You just review your listings and then, with a few mouse clicks, choose which ones you want to upload. This makes it quick and easy to list products that you sell repeatedly.

Creating Click Here Links

In Chapter 9, we discussed the methods for creating "bait" listings to attract buyers. Then, within your bait listing, you send the buyer to your store using Click Here links. Here are the steps required with Turbo Lister to easily create a Click Here link in your listing:

1. Open Turbo Lister, select your listing, and then click the **Description Builder** button.

2. Open your web browser, login to eBay, and go to your eBay Store. (Click the **door** icon next to your User ID.)

3. Click on the **category** (or specific item) where you want the buyer to land.

4. Go to the top of your browser and left-click once on the entire Internet address displayed. (This highlights the URL of the item or category.)

5. Right-click your mouse and select **copy.** (You are copying the entire URL address.)

6. Close or minimize your browser. You are now back to the Turbo Lister item description screen.

7. Place your cursor where you want to insert the hyperlink. (Position the mouse and then left-click it.)

8. At the top of the Turbo Lister tool bar, click on the **world globe** icon and infinity looking button. (It looks like a globe with two infinity chain links.)

9. An Insert Hyperlink window box opens with two blank fields. In the **Text to Display** field, type **Click Here.**

10. In the **Address** field, left-click once to place your cursor in that field box. Then right-click the mouse and choose **paste.** (This will paste the URL you previously copied to where you want the customer to land.)

11. Select **Insert.** Your link is inserted into your listing where you had previously designated.

That's it! You have just placed a Click Here hyperlink that will land your customer exactly in the category or on the specific item that you want in your eBay Store. Want to test it?

At the top of Turbo Lister, you will see three View tabs. You are currently under Design View. Click on the **Preview** tab, and you will see what your listing will look like. Scroll down to where you placed your hyperlink and select **Click Here.** It should have landed exactly where you designated.

Sales Reports

EBay provides a free tracking report for your monthly sales. Studying these reports provides useful insights as to what products are selling, when they are selling, and what prices they bring. You can use the sales reports not only to analyze your sales but also to help you modify your listing elements and timing.

There are two types of online statements, Sales Reports and Sales Reports Plus. The following information is provided in the basic Sales Report:

- Total sales
- Ended listings
- Successful listings (number and percent)
- Average sales price per product
- Net eBay fees
- Net PayPal fees

Sales Reports Plus provides further analysis of your monthly sales. It provides all the information of Sales Reports plus the following:

- The number of unique buyers
- Metrics by category
- Metrics by listing format (Auction-Style, Fixed Price, Store Inventory)
- Metrics by ending day and time
- Detailed and summary eBay fees

Both versions of Sales Reports are free. You can view them from your My eBay page under My Subscriptions. Sign up for the Sales Reports by selecting the **Help** link, typing **sales reports** in the search field, and then selecting **Sales Reports—Subscribing and Unsubscribing.**

Store Traffic Reports

If you have an eBay Store, you will have access to valuable sales information from eBay's Store Traffic Reports. These reports allow you to monitor and analyze the activities of your store. Of significant importance is the ability to find where your buyers originate (eBay or the Internet), what search engines sent them to you, and what pages and products are the most popular. The Store Traffic Reports include the following:

- **Visits Report:** Identifies which sites and search engines your visitors are coming from and the keywords they are using to find you.

- **Unique Visitor Report:** Shows the number of unique visitors who visited your store during the last month. Each person is counted only once no matter how many times they visit.

- **Search Keywords Report:** Lists all keywords the visitor used to find your store. You can use this report to find which keywords are most effective in your listing titles.

- **Store Search Keywords Report:** Identifies which keywords are the ones most frequently used to search for items within your store.

- **Page Views Report:** Tracks the number of times visitors have viewed certain items in your store.

- **Most Popular Pages Report:** Identifies which products and pages your buyers are viewing.

- **Popular Listings Report:** Displays the number of times each listing has been viewed, revealing your most popular items.

- **Store Home Page Views Report:** Shows the number of times your store's home page has been viewed.

- **Referring Domains Reports:** Reveals the websites that your visitors were visiting immediately before accessing your store. You can then determine how visitors are finding you.

- **Search Engine Report:** Identifies which search engines your buyers are using to locate your store and listings. Use this report to determine which search engines are sending you the most customers.

Auction Management Software

Your business may grow to the point where you need help from business management software. You should know that there are several third-party vendors that provide eBay-centric business software.

Located in the eBay Solutions Directory is a list of certified providers that have been approved by eBay. To find the directory, click the **Site Map** and then look under Seller Tools. This directory provides users of these products a way to leave comments and feedback about the products. You should look here before you decide on any one application.

The following are some of the more popular eBay auction management software applications from third-party vendors. They are listed in alphabetical order and are noted as either desktop-based or web-based products. I do not personally endorse any particular application in the list. The list is provided simply as a starting point for your investigation when you are ready to upgrade to eBay auction management software. Most of these management companies offer a 30-day or longer free trial, so try out a few before deciding on one.

- Auction Hawk: www.auctionhawk.com (web)
- Auction Sage: www.auctionsagesoftware.com (desktop)
- Auction Wizard 2000: www.auctionwizard2000.com (desktop)
- Auctiva: www.auctiva.com (web)
- DEK Auction Manager: www.dekauctionmanager.com (desktop)
- Infopia: www.infopia.com (web)
- MarketplaceAdvisor: www.channeladvisor.com/mw (web)
- Spoonfeeder: www.spoonfeeder.com (web)
- Vendio: www.vendio.com (web)
- Zoovy: www.zoovy.com (web)

The Adventure Begins

When I first started selling on eBay, I needed a book just like this. Out of necessity I developed, refined, and still use the methodology herein. At times I have alluded to some of my mistakes and misjudgments about product selection, listing creation, and excess inventory so that you can avoid making the same mistakes. I have also shared my most successful techniques and strategies. Believe me, you will save time, effort, frustration, and money when you eliminate the guesswork and follow the methodology outlined in this book.

Now you know what many eBay professionals know and do. It is my genuine wish that you benefit from this book and experience the possibilities and satisfaction of also becoming an eBay profit maker!

How to Use Instant Market Research

Instant Market Research (IMR) is an essential tool, developed by Worldwide Brands (WWB), that provides Internet marketplace research information invaluable to all online sellers. You will use IMR in your methodology to generate product ideas, find niches and ideal niches, determine the probability of success for selling your products, analyze the competition, and then locate reputable suppliers for your products.

The information provided by IMR is generated mostly from Internet data, not just eBay data. Internet data is equally important, however, in determining the online marketplace supply, demand, and competition for your products. The information provided from the overall online marketplace is directly relevant to selling on eBay. Many eBay buyers, in fact, begin their product search not on eBay but on the Internet. Many times your competition is on the Internet, not on eBay. Without Internet marketplace analysis, you will not have a complete picture of your online competition and therefore cannot determine your products' potential for success on eBay.

Worldwide Brands includes all of its analysis tools (including IMR) and access to its supplier databases in the Product Sourcing Membership package. This is not a monthly subscription, but a one-time fee for a lifetime membership giving you access to all of these tools. You can receive a discount coupon on a lifetime membership at www.worldwidebrands.com/studentrate.

Note that the specific steps presented in this appendix are current and accurate when this book was written. WWB may choose to change their site at any time with new features and services. Regardless, the procedures presented here will provide a basic understanding for how to conduct fundamental product analysis even if some specific steps have changed. Be sure to review the video tutorials WWB provides on their site before you begin your analysis.

Generate Product Ideas

Use the process described here when you want to generate product ideas. With this method, you will be able to determine which brand name items have the potential to become one of your products. Record your findings on your #1. Product Idea Worksheet (discussed in Chapters 3 and 4 and downloadable from www.trainingu4auctions. com/notebook).

Step 1. Category Search

Perform a category search as follows:

1. Login to your Worldwide Brands account and select the **Find Products Now** button.

2. Under the **View All** section, click the **Brands** link.

3. At the bottom of the page, set the **Results per page** drop-down menu to **100**.

4. A list of product brand names will appear in alphabetical order. You can jump to other products quickly by selecting the first letter of the product name in the **Brand Names by Alphabet** section.

5. Scroll the list, looking for interesting product ideas. Be sure to click the **Next** button at the bottom of the page to view more results.

6. When you find a brand name product of interest, click the active link of the product name.

Step 2. Analysis

You are now viewing a quick analysis for that product. At this stage in the methodology, you are only interested in two factors: a good chance of success and a good source of suppliers. These are provided in the Suppliers tab.

1. Click the **Suppliers** tab.

2. In the **Marketplace Research Results** bar, the product must have at least a 60 percent chance (the "good" or "best" range) of success.

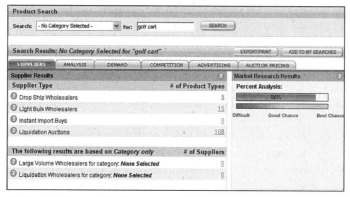

Marketplace Research Results

3. Under **Supplier Results,** it is best if there is more than one product supplier. While only one is not a showstopper, more than one supplier is preferred. Several suppliers are ideal.

4. Now review the **Market Research Results** bar. Any brand name that does not meet the 60 percent threshold should probably not be considered as a good potential product.

Any brand-name products you are interested in selling that meet your criteria should be recorded on your #1. Product Idea Worksheet. In this phase, remember that you are only generating product ideas. You will further analyze the specific products later in the methodology.

Analyze a Product

When you have a particular product that you are interested in selling, you need to conduct further detailed analysis. Use the steps here to determine the demand, competition, supply, and overall probability that the product will be successful.

Step 1. Conduct a Product Search

Perform a product search as follows:

1. In the **Search** drop-down menu, select the **Category** link for the product you are interested in selling. If you are unsure, just leave it as **No Category Selected.**

2. Type the primary keywords of the product in the **for:** field.

3. Click the **Search** button.

4. When the results are presented, click the **Auction Pricing** tab.

5. You are now looking at all of the listings on eBay that have the same product keywords in their title. Scan this list of products, checking for outliers (listings that are related, but not relevant, to your product). Narrow your search by adding more pertinent keywords and conduct a new product search. Continue this process until you have narrowed the search to the particular product you want to sell. Now click the **Supplier** tab.

Step 2. Interpret the Supplier Tab

The **Supplier Results** section should have a few suppliers listed. Also check the **Category Only** results toward the bottom of the suppliers. Click the active link number that is next to the supplier type. You will be taken immediately to a list of all suppliers for that product. You can then click on a particular supplier to learn more or even to set up an account.

If the supplier list is short, it may be difficult to find a good source for the product. However, this is not a showstopper. It just means that there are few suppliers of this product in Worldwide Brands's databases, and you will need to contact the manufacturer on your own to find a wholesaler.

Step 3. Interpret the Analysis Tab

The **Marketplace Research Results** bar is determined by a mathematical algorithm that compares online demand, competition, and advertising for your product. It provides a combined overall score that allows you to make a well-informed decision as to whether you will be able to sell this product successfully online.

For our methodology, the bar should be about 60 percent or better. If the percentage score is less than 60, the product is probably not worth investigating further. Move on to the next product. Be sure that you are using the best keywords for the product. If results are poor, alter the keywords slightly and conduct the same search again.

Also, remember that this is to be used for a high-level analysis. Sometimes a specific product analysis may produce a less-than-desirable score while an overall category may pass the test. If your specific product search has failed the test, back up a level and see if that product's category passes the test. If you feel further analysis is warranted for a specific brand-name item, use the methodology described later to analyze a product.

Step 4. Interpret the Demand Tab

You can interpret the Demand tab by doing the following:

1. Click the **Demand** tab.

2. Set the **Results per page** menu to **100**.

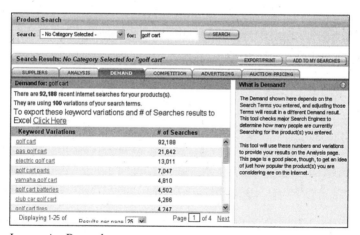

Interpreting Demand

This report analyzes data from the major search engines to reveal how many searches are being made for the product. You will then see just how popular the product is online. While I have no set criteria for demand, if the product is getting more than 1,000 searches, it is a popular product with good online demand.

Step 5. Interpret the Competition Tab

The competition report reveals how many other online sellers have listings that use the same product name. You will see separate numbers for Yahoo!, Google, and eBay. The results will vary widely depending on how much you have narrowed your search when selecting your keywords.

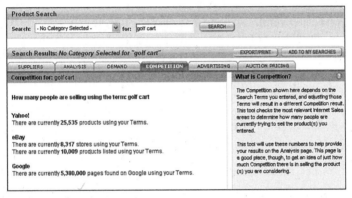

Interpreting Competition

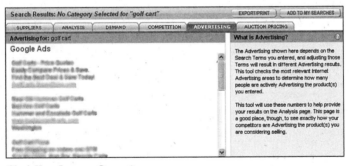

Check Your Internet Competitors

You want relatively low competition to avoid entering a marketplace that is already saturated. There is no set number to look for, but the less competition the better. If you find that there are several hundred stores or sellers on eBay that are selling your product, you have considerable competition and should move on to another product that has less. Ideally, I would prefer to have fewer than 100 eBay competitors. Fewer than 50 is even better and so on.

Step 6. Interpret the Advertising Tab

With the Advertising tab, you can spy on your Internet competitors. This report will reveal Google ads that are for the product you want to sell. Click the links and study your Internet competitors' websites. You can read their descriptions and discover their selling prices. (Remember never to copy anyone else's descriptions.)

You will discover other items that they sell that you may be interested in. You are not necessarily looking for a pass/fail analysis with this tab. It is mostly used for information gathering to help determine how to properly list your product on eBay.

Find Reputable Product Suppliers

Once you have determined which products you will sell, use this process to find reputable suppliers of the products. Worldwide Brands maintains several databases with hundreds of drop shippers, wholesalers, importers, and other suppliers. To qualify for database inclusion, each supplier must pass a stringent investigation and analysis. If a company meets the WWB criteria and is approved, you are assured that you will be dealing with a reputable supplier.

Step 1. Find Your Supplier

Unless I am looking specifically for a drop shipper, I like to start my search with Light-Bulk Wholesalers. These are suppliers that have agreed to sell their items for a smaller minimum order quantity than larger wholesalers require. If there are no Light-Bulk Wholesalers, then I conduct the search again and this time select Large-Volume or Liquidation Wholesalers.

1. Close the previous search screen and open a new screen from WWB's member page by clicking the **Find Products Now** button.

2. Under the **View All** section, click the **Suppliers** tab.

3. Using the **Search** drop-down menu, select the type of supplier you want. Your choices are as follows:

   - Drop Ship Wholesalers
   - Light-Bulk Wholesalers

- Large-Volume Wholesalers
- Liquidation Wholesalers

4. In the **for:** field, type the keywords for the type of product you want to sell.

5. You can also choose to show only suppliers that ship internationally or the 30 most recently added suppliers. This will help you find new suppliers with new product possibilities.

6. Click the **Search** button.

7. Set the **Results per page** to **100.**

You can now view all suppliers for the product based on the type of supplier you choose. This page also reveals whether the suppliers offer more than one type of service and if they will ship internationally.

In some cases, a supplier search will not produce any suppliers for your product. This does not mean there is not a supplier for the product. It just means that there were no suppliers that passed WWB's test for database inclusion. If you decide to proceed with selling this particular product, you will need to contact the manufacturer to find a wholesaler. Proceed with some caution, as these suppliers may have higher minimum order quantities or may not be as willing to work with eBay sellers as those approved by WWB.

Step 2. Apply Online to Become a Dealer

Here are the steps to apply online to become a dealer:

1. Click the link for the supplier you are interested in.

2. You will see contact information and a website (if available) to learn more about the supplier. Scroll down to see the brand names and types of products this supplier stocks.

3. If you wish to set up an account with the supplier, scroll to the **Online Account Setup** page, enter the required information in any fields missing data, and click the **Submit** button. You will usually hear from the supplier with new account approval status notification within one to two weeks.

If you start the process to become a dealer and notice that a business license or reseller certificate is required and you do not yet have a license, don't let that deter you. It is quite a simple and inexpensive process to obtain a business license and reseller certificate. Read about the benefits of licensure in Chapter 12.

This appendix is only a synopsis of the ability you will have to find, analyze, and select products that you will feel confident selling. Spend some time delving into what a WWB Product Sourcing Membership and analysis tools can do for you.

How to Use HammerTap

HammerTap is a comprehensive eBay marketplace analysis tool. It is used by serious sellers to eliminate the guesswork of product selection and listing creation. Use HammerTap to conduct the profitability analysis for the products you will be researching.

This appendix is not a tutorial for how to use HammerTap. The application is multifaceted and can perform more detailed analysis than is required for our methodology. We will only review the specific steps that are required to produce the reports used for our methodology. Note also that the steps presented in this appendix were current when the book was written. Future software upgrades could change the specific steps required. However, the procedures in this book will still provide an understanding for how to conduct eBay marketplace research for any product you are thinking of selling on eBay.

You can receive a free trial and a discount on the monthly subscription at www.hammertap.com/studentrate. After you sign up, complete the video lessons for how to use the product. In particular, take the HammerTap Tutorials and the Using the Product Search video tutorials. Once you have completed these lessons, the information in this chapter will be more easily understood.

Quick Analysis

Use the Quick Analysis steps to see if an item is worth investigating further as a potential product. This analysis will provide a pass/fail score to help you quickly narrow the product ideas on your #1. Product Idea Worksheet (as discussed in Chapters 3 and 4).

In addition, use this process when you are doing a quick search of new products, such as reviewing liquidations sites. When you find a product of interest, perform a Quick Analysis. Either the product fails or it is worthy of further research.

Note that if a product passes a Quick Analysis, it does not mean you should choose that product to sell on eBay. This is only one step in the analysis. However, if the product fails this test, you can stop any further research for that product. Therefore, the Quick Analysis test is the first hurdle. If the product passes, move on to the next step of the methodology. If it fails, move on to the next product.

Conduct Quick Analysis

There seems to be many steps for Quick Analysis. Actually, the time required to accomplish this is only two to three minutes. After you have performed this analysis a few times, you will be able to zip through it quickly. Best of all, using this process, you will be able to determine in less than three minutes whether one of your product ideas is worth pursuing.

Step 1. Create a Search Preview

Perform the following steps to create a search preview:

1. Login to HammerTap.

2. Click the **Product Search** button.

3. Enter the primary keywords of the product.

4. Choose **All of these words** from the drop-down menu.

5. Select the **Current Auctions** and enter the date range for the last **90 days.**

6. Set **Number of Auctions** to **500.**

7. Select **Regular, Fixed,** and **Store** items.

8. Click **Search Preview.**

At this point, check to be sure the total number of listings is less than 500. If it is at 500, then you need to back up a step and increase the number of auctions to the next highest increment. Continue this process until the total number of listings returned is less than the number you selected. Then click **Search Preview** again.

The preview report will give you an overview of the products found on eBay with your keywords. When scanning the report, you will find that not all listings will be relevant to the specific product you want to sell. For example, if you are selling an iPod, your keywords will also produce listings for iPod cases. Since you are not selling the case, including it in your analysis would skew your results. Scan this list to see what listings have keywords that you need to exclude.

Step 2. Narrow Your Search

To narrow your search, perform the following steps:

1. Enter the keywords you want to eliminate in the **Exclude Keywords** field.

2. Click **Search Preview** and review the list again.

3. Continue this process until you have narrowed your search to the specific product you want to sell.

4. Once you have your keywords and excluded keywords set, click **Start Search.**

Your Findings report will appear. Check the report for accuracy by double-checking your keywords for typos.

Sometimes a seller with the same keywords has included other items, or several of the same item, in the listing (selling a quantity greater than one). Including these listings in your analysis would provide misleading results. You now need to remove any of these outliers (any listing outside of the scope of your item).

Step 3. Remove the Outliers

Follow these steps to remove the outliers:

1. Click the **Listings** button at the bottom of the page.

2. Scroll down the **Titles** column looking for more keywords that you may want to eliminate. If you find any, click the **Edit Search** button, add those keywords to exclusion list, and conduct a new search.

3. Click the **High Bid** column and arrange the list in descending order (arrow pointing down).

4. Scroll down the **Total Sales** column to find the first few products that sold. Check that their prices are not out of line with all other sales. Check also the **Quantity Sold** column to be sure that only one item sold.

5. Remove any high-priced outliers from the search data by unchecking the **Include** checkbox for that item.

remove the outliers

Remove the Outliers

6. Now sort the **High Bid** column in ascending order (arrow pointing up).

7. Remove any low-priced outliers from the search data by unchecking the **Include** checkbox for that item. (You can also eliminate any "no sales" in your original search by adding a **Minimum Price** to your search).

8. Click the **Filter the Report** button at the top of the screen.

You have now narrowed the search using keywords to exclude and have removed any outliers that could give misleading data. Your filtered report will now provide only the information that is relevant for your specific product.

Step 4. Interpret the Report

In the Results section of the report, observe the listing success rate (LSR) percentage.

Results		Listing Success Rate (LSR)
Total Listings	113	73.45 %
Listings with Sale	83	
Listing Success Rate (LSR)	73.45%	
Average Sales Price (ASP)	$105.19	
Total Sales	$10,413.49	
Sellers with Sale	48	
Average Sales Per Seller	2.06	26.55 %
Average Revenue Per Seller	$216.95	☐ Listings With Sale ☐ Listings W/Out Sale

Product Search Results

The LSR is your product's first hurdle. It is the sell-through rate. For example, if 100 particular items were listed on eBay and 70 sold, this means the product has a 70 percent chance of selling. For our methodology, the bar must be at least 60 percent. If the Percent Sold bar is less than 60, the product has failed the test. Move on to the next product.

I consider an excellent LSR to be over 75 percent. Any LSR that is over 90 percent is a likely candidate for an ideal niche and deserves special attention and documentation in your methodology.

If the **Percent Sold** score is above 60, the product has passed the first hurdle and is worthy of further analysis. Therefore, you now need to determine what you expect the product to sell for on eBay.

1. Scroll down toward the bottom to the column that is labeled **ASP** (average sales price).

2. Record the price where the **ASP** column meets the **End Day** row.

Do not use the average sales price from the Results section. It is an average price that you will be able to surpass using our methodology. I have found that a more accurate price predictor is the **ASP** in the row **End Day**. That ASP price then will be your expected selling price to record on your #1. Product Idea Worksheet.

Caution When Interpreting the Results

Sometimes the results you receive can be skewed by various factors. This is especially true when the number of listings used to generate the data is a low number.

For example, say you are going to sell a LeSportSac travel tote bag. You conduct your Quick Analysis and find that the initial numbers returned in the report look great. It has an acceptable ASP and 100 percent LSR. However, you also need to look at the number of listings that were used to create the data. In actuality, maybe only two bags were listed during the time frame you searched.

Since only two bags were listed, the fact that two bags sold will give you the 100 percent LSR. However, this sample size means almost nothing statistically. It is the same as rolling the dice twice and each time it comes up a lucky seven. Could you then make a prediction that all dice tossed will produce a seven? No, the sample size is too small.

Now let's look at the ASP using the same example. The ASP for the bag is $50. This looks great until you search for the outliers. That is, when you discover that there were only two bags sold. One sold for $1 and one sold for $100. The ASP of $50 is not meaningful now.

I like to have a sample size (number of listings sold) of at least 100 before I begin to feel comfortable with the numbers. But the larger the sample size the better—assuming you have removed your outliers.

Detailed eBay Market Research

When you have a product that you are ready to list on eBay, you should conduct detailed eBay market research in order to determine how to create the listing. Using this method, you will find the sellers with the best performing listings of your product and learn what particular enhancements and tweaking of the listing will improve the selling price and sell-through rate. This removes the guesswork and will help you with the questions you will need to answer during listing creation. In particular, HammerTap will answer these questions for you:

1. What are my chances of selling this product?

2. How much should it sell for?

3. Which Listing Type is the best to use?

4. What End Day and End Hour will increase my ASP?

5. Which Listing Duration should I use?

6. What should my Starting Price be?

7. What are the best Keywords to use in my title?

8. Will Listing Enhancements or Upgrades increase the price for this item?

Questions 1 and 2 are answered by performing the Quick Analysis procedure previously presented. Therefore, you will need to perform the Quick Analysis first before you are able to answer the remaining questions.

To answer questions 3 through 6, you have to decide which is more important: a higher selling price or a higher sell-through rate. For me, I already know my sell-through rate (listing success rate) will be acceptable because I always perform a Quick Analysis on my potential products before I ever purchase them. My goal then is to maximize my selling price. Therefore, when answering questions 3 through 6, we will be focusing on the ASP column.

To answer questions 3 through 6:

1. Scroll to the bottom of the Quick Analysis report to the **Option** column.

2. Under the **Option** column, go to the row of the question you want answered.

3. Scroll to the right to where the row and **ASP** intersect.

4. The left-hand **ASP** column will contain the answers to each question.

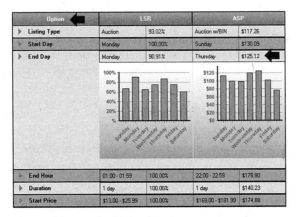

Answer Questions for Listing Creation

Once again, double-check the total number of listings and remove the outliers. This will ensure that your data is not skewed and that you are not making important product purchasing or listing decisions based on faulty data.

To answer questions 7 and 8 (Keywords and Enhancements), deeper analysis is required. Do not depend on the results in the summary findings report. Instead you need to click the buttons titled **Which Listing Enhancements Should I Use?** and **What Title Keywords Should I Use?** I will not repeat the steps for this analysis since it has been thoroughly documented in HammerTap's training tutorials. Instead, watch the video tutorials for each particular search.

When you conduct the Listing Enhancements search, your decision will be based on whether the enhancements will increase the ASP of your product enough to justify the additional cost. Use the following guide to compare the eBay fees for enhancements to the price increase you can expect from using them.

You should always check the current eBay fees for this process. Go to eBay.com and select the **Help** link. Type **ebay.com fees,** then scroll down to **Optional feature fees.** The eBay enhancement (listing upgrade) fees at the time of this writing are as follows:

Buy It Now: Adds a Buy It Now option to an Auction-Style listing.

Buy It Now Price	Fee
$1.00–$9.99	$0.05
$10.00–$24.99	$0.10
$25.00–$49.99	$0.20
$50.00 or more	$0.25

Reserve: Requires that a minimum price is met before the item can be sold.

Reserve Price	Fee
$0.01–$199.99	$2.00
$200.00 and up	1% of reserve price (up to $50.00)

Bold: $1.00—Bold the title.

Border: $3.00—Places a border around the title.

Gift Services: 25 cents—A gift icon will appear next to your title, indicating that you offer gift wrapping.

Highlight: $5.00—Uses a background color to highlight the title.

Featured Plus!: Places your listing in the featured section above standard listings for items in the same category.

Featured Plus! Price	Fee
$0.01–$24.99	$9.95
$25.00–$199.99	$14.95
$200.00–$499.99	$19.95
$500.00 or more	$24.95

Gallery Featured: $19.95—Places your listing above the general picture gallery.

Category Search

Use HammerTap's Category Search feature when you want to generate product ideas by browsing various categories. This process will help you quickly find the top-performing products in a particular category.

Searching a category for 30 days can produce a lot of data. Therefore, it is important to eliminate as many of the outlier listings as possible. For example, if you know you do not want to sell any items that are less than $20, set the minimum price to $20. I also like to set a maximum price appropriate for the category I am searching. This helps eliminate multiple quantity listings.

Step 1. Initial Category Search

To perform the initial category search:

1. Click the **Category Search** button at the very top.

2. Enter the **Category Number** if you know it or use the **Category Picker** button to work down from major categories to the particular subcategory of interest.

3. Select **Current Auctions** and enter the date range for the last **30 days.**

4. Set **Number of Auctions** to **10,000.**

5. Set your **Minimum** or **Maximum** price range.

6. Select **Regular, BIN Only,** and **Store** items.

7. Click **Start Search.**

At this point, check to be sure the total number of listings is less than 10,000. If it is at 10,000, you need to back up a step and increase the **Number of Auctions** to the next highest increment. Continue this process until the total number of listings returned is less than the number you selected. Then click **Search** again.

It can sometimes take a couple of minutes for HammerTap to search 10,000 listings. Wait for the spinning ball to stop and the Findings report to appear before you proceed to Step 2.

Step 2. Quick Keyword Search

To perform the quick keyword search:

1. In the section What Do I Want Answered?, click the button titled **What Title Keywords Should I Use?**

2. Under **Filter Report,** type **60** in the **Minimum % Sold** field.

3. Type **100** in the **Minimum Number of Listings** field. (If your results are small for the category you are researching, leave this field blank.)

4. Type an appropriate price in the **Minimum Average Price** field if you want to eliminate items with lower selling prices.

5. In the **Sort By** drop-down menu, select **# of Listings.**

6. Click the **Filter** button.

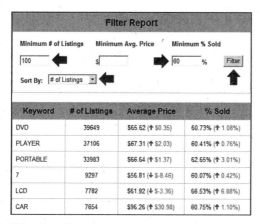

Filter Your Keywords

Now scan through the results table looking for keywords of products, especially brand names. The keywords for the top-selling items in that category will be revealed. Now repeat Step 2, but this time sort by **Average Price.** Write all product ideas discovered on your #1. Product Idea Worksheet.

Optional Step 3. Search Detailed Keyword Report

If you find a hot or very promising category, use this report to drill down further into the keywords to search for products.

1. At the bottom of the page, click the **Keywords** button.

2. Scroll to the right, left-click and hold the **ASP/Item** column heading, then drag and drop the column just to the right of **# of Auctions** column.

3. Use the same process to drag and drop the **Average # of Bids** column just to the right of the **ASP/Item** column.

4. Use the same process to drag and drop the **Auction Success Rate** column just to the right of the **Average # of Bids** column.

5. Click the column heading labeled **ASP/Item** until the report is sorted in descending order (arrow pointing down).

	Keyword	# of Auctions	ASP/Item ▽	Average # of Bids	Auction Success Rate
1	PMPPVR	4	$300.00	0.25	25.00 %
2	ANALOG	4	$300.00	0.25	25.00 %
3	LX110	1	$300.00	1.00	100.00 %
4	NEWEXTRAS	1	$299.99	5.00	100.00 %
5	SONOS	1	$295.00	12.00	100.00 %
6	ZP80	1	$295.00	12.00	100.00 %
7	7200RPM	3	$295.00	0.00	100.00 %
8	REMOTES	1	$284.00	12.00	100.00 %
9	FREEVIEWTV	32	$265.11	0.63	46.88 %
10	WD	31	$264.00	0.00	12.90 %

Detailed Keyword Search

At this point, the first five columns should be as follows:

- Keyword
- # of Auctions
- ASP/Item
- Average # of Bids
- Auction Success Rate

You are now looking at a very valuable report. Scroll down the list looking at these four columns to identify the top financial (ASP/Item) and sell-through (Auction Success Rate) performers. Be sure to check the # of Auctions column so that you are not looking at just one auction.

Now see which keywords are associated with the top performers. Product ideas will then jump out at you. Record them on your #1. Product Idea Worksheet. If you find that the Auction Success Rate is low for the top-selling items, you may be in a category that is saturated.

Find Your Giant Competitors

Use this method to find the sellers that have the best-performing listings, or your giant competitors, of a particular product on eBay.

1. Select the **Product Search** button at the very top.

2. Enter the keywords of the product you want to sell.

3. Select **Current Auctions** and enter the date range for the last 90 days.

4. Set **Number of Auctions** to **500.**

5. Select **Regular, BIN Only,** and **Store** items.

6. Click **Search Preview** and be sure that these listings are the products for which you want to find the top sellers.

7. Narrow your search by entering the keywords to exclude.

8. Click **Start Search.** You are now viewing all the listings for these products on eBay in the last 90 days.

9. At the very bottom of the screen, click the **Listings** button.

10. Click the column heading labeled **Total Sales** until the report is sorted in descending order (arrow pointing down).

Scroll down the list looking at the Title column. You will find many products that have the exact same title. Most of these will also have the same Total Sales price. These products are most likely listed by the same seller. Click on one of these titles. You will now see the completed listing exactly as it appeared on eBay. This listing will reveal the seller's User ID.

Spy on Your Giant Competitors

The Seller Search feature is useful when you want to investigate a particular seller. Use this feature when spying on your top or giant sellers to find their most successful products in the last 30 days.

In order to investigate sellers, you will need their eBay User IDs. If you are not sure who your giant competitors are, see the preceding section.

Step 1. Find the Giant's Listings

Follow these steps to find the Giant's listings:

1. Click the **Seller Search** button at the top of the page.

2. Enter the seller's **User ID** in the **eBay Seller ID** field.

3. Select **Current Auctions** and enter the date range for the last **30 days.**

4. Set **Number of Auctions** to **500.**

5. Select **Regular, BIN Only,** and **Store** items.

6. Click **Start Search.**

7. When the report appears, click the **Listings** button at the bottom of the report.

8. Click the column heading labeled **Total Sales** until the report is sorted in descending order (arrow pointing down).

You now need to sort the same report further.

Step 2. Perform Secondary Sorts

To perform the secondary sorts, complete the following steps:

1. Place your cursor over the **Total Sales** column, left-click and hold the mouse, then drag and drop the column into the gray area directly above.

2. Ensure that the **Total Sales** column has the arrow pointing down.

3. Use the same process to drag and drop the **Quantity Sold** column to the gray area. Ensure that the arrow is pointing down.

4. Use the same process to drag and drop the **Title** column to the gray area. Ensure that the arrow is pointing down.

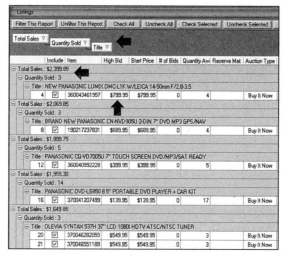

Create Multiquery Search

You are now looking at a multilevel sorting hierarchy of the most successful selling products for that seller. However, at this point, the details are hidden.

Step 3. Reveal the Products

To reveal the products, complete the following:

1. For the first **Total Sales** listing, click the **+** (plus) button.

2. Continue clicking the **+** (plus) buttons down the sort hierarchy for this item until all buttons read **–** (minus).

You will now see the **Total Sales, Total Quantity Sold,** and **Title** for this seller's most successful product. Repeat Step 3 for all remaining top-selling products. When you see that the quantity numbers are getting low, you are no longer looking at their top-selling products.

Product Development Notebook

All of the worksheets used for your methodology should be organized and placed in your Product Development Notebook. A coversheet is provided to easily identify your notebook and to provide contact information in case it is lost. Place this coversheet in the plastic sleeve on the front of your three-ring binder.

The worksheets, as well as the other forms and checklists mentioned in this book, are available for download free of charge at www. trainingu4auctions.com/notebook. These sheets are not copyrighted, and you can make as many copies as you need.

Product Development Notebook

Book # _____

Name: _____

If found, please call (_____) _____

Notebook Coversheet

#1. Product Idea Worksheet (Manual)

List all product ideas below. Use additional lines if necessary.

Product Idea Keywords Category	Manufacturer Contact Information (*name, phone, website, e-mail, blog*)	Competition Total # Listed on eBay	Total Sold (*Green Prices*)	Sell-Through Percent (*Sold ÷ Listed*)	Average Selling Price (*ASP*)	Passed All Tests ✓

#1. Product Idea Worksheet (Manual)

#1. Product Idea Worksheet (Analysis Tools)

List all product ideas below. Use additional lines if necessary.

Product Idea Keywords Category	Manufacturer Contact Information *(name, phone, website, e-mail, blog)*	H. Tap ASP *(End Day)*	H. Tap LSR%	IMR Market Bar %, ☐ Ideal Niche	IMR Passed Demand Test ✓	IMR Passed Comp. Test ✓ ☐ <20	Passed All Tests ✓
				☐		☐	
				☐		☐	
				☐		☐	
				☐		☐	
				☐		☐	
				☐		☐	
				☐		☐	
				☐		☐	
				☐		☐	
				☐		☐	
				☐		☐	
				☐		☐	
				☐		☐	

#1. Product Idea Worksheet (Analysis Tools)

#2. Giant Competitor Spy Worksheet (Manual)

List all product ideas below. Use additional lines if necessary.

Giant Competitor User ID: _____

Product Idea and Keywords	Category and Subcategories	Competition Total # Listed on eBay	Total Sold (*Green Prices*)	Sell-Through Percent (*Sold ÷ Listed*)	Average Selling Price (*ASP*)	Multiple Seller Check ✓	Passed All Tests ✓

#2. Giant Competitor Spy Worksheet (Analysis Tools)

List all product ideas below. Use additional lines if necessary.

Giant Competitor User ID: _____

Product Idea and Keywords	Categories and Subcategories	H. Tap ASP (End Day)	H. Tap LSR%	IMR Market Bar %, ☐ Ideal Niche	IMR Passed Demand Test ✓	IMR Passed Comp. Test ✓ ☐ <20	Passed All Tests ✓
				☐		☐	
				☐		☐	
				☐		☐	
				☐		☐	
				☐		☐	
				☐		☐	
				☐		☐	
				☐		☐	
				☐		☐	
				☐		☐	
				☐		☐	

#2. Giant Competitor Spy Worksheet (Analysis Tools)

#3. Product Profitability Worksheet

List all qualified products from Worksheet #1 or #2. Use two lines if necessary.
Your minimum Profit Margin Requirement is __25%__ *(25% is suggested)*
Your minimum Profit Requirement is __$10__ *($10 is suggested)*

A. Product Name	B. Avg. Selling Price (ASP)	C. Retail MSRP (Manuf. Website)	D. Est. Cost (C × 50%)	E. eBay and PayPal Fees (B × Fee%)	F. Profit B − (D + E)	G. Margin% (F ÷ B) × 100	H. Meets Min. Profit ✓	I. Meets Min. Margin ✓	J. Passed Product Eval. Test ✓	K. Passed All Tests ✓ ☐ I. Niche ☐ < 20
										☐ I.N. ☐ < 20
										☐ I.N. ☐ < 20
										☐ I.N. ☐ < 20
										☐ I.N. ☐ < 20
										☐ I.N. ☐ < 20
										☐ I.N. ☐ < 20

#3. Product Profitability Worksheet

#4. Product Supplier Worksheet

List all qualified products from #3; transfer contact info from your #1. Product Idea Worksheet or from Instant Market Research.

Your Approved Product	Supplier Contact Information (name, phone, website, e-mail)	Type of Supplier (Wholesaler, Light Bulk, Drop Shipper, Liquidator, etc.)	Dealer App. Requested ✓	Dealer App. Sent ✓	Supplier Interview Completed ✓	Product Ordered ✓

#4. Product Supplier Worksheet

 **Resources**

I have provided links to some of the most useful resources for eBay sellers. They are grouped alphabetically by category and then by the most often used links within that category. Note that a link map such as **eBay>help>type: fees** means to go to eBay's homepage, select the **Help** link, and then type **fees** in the search box.

Antique Sites

To conduct research on antiques:

- www.goantiques.com
- www.tias.com
- www.priceminer.com

Business License

Incorporation service providers:

- www.legalzoom.com/studentrate
- www.bizfilings.com/studentrate

eBay

eBay registration:

- www.ebay.com

eBay help:

- eBay>help
- eBay>site map
- eBay>live help

Phone support for PowerSellers and eBay storeowners only:

- eBay>help>contact us

eBay Express:

- www.ebayexpress.com

eBay disputes:

- eBay>site map>dispute console
- www.squaretrade.com

eBay Stores:

- http://pages.ebay.com/storefronts/start.html

eBay, Other Helpful Links

eBay Toolbar:

- http://pages.ebay.com/ebay_toolbar/

eBay Seller Central:

- eBay>site map>seller central

eBay blogs:

- http://blogs.ebay.com/ebaynii@ebay.com

eBay discussion boards, My World:

- eBay>site map>connect

eBay Main Street:

- eBay>site map>more community programs> mainstreet—government relations

Selling specialty services:

- http://pages.ebay.com/sellercentral/specialtyservices

To find local eBay education courses:

- www.poweru.net/ebay/student/searchindex.asp

Keyword Finding Tools

- http://pulse.ebay.com
- http://keyword.ebay.com
- https://adwords.google.com/select/KeywordToolExternal
- "Yahoo! Keyword Finder" at http://tinyurl.com/58y7c5
- www.wordtracker.com
- www.typobid.com (finds commonly misspelled keywords)

PayPal

PayPal registration:

- www.paypal.com

Live PayPal representative phone support:

- For Premier and Business levels only: 1-888-221-1161
- For other members: 402-935-2050

Photography

Photography research and reviews:

- www.cnet.com
- www.dpreview.com
- www.calumetphoto.com
- www.photoflex.com

Cloud Dome, Infinity Boards, Cubes:

- www.trainingu4auctions.com
- www.trainingu4auctions.net (eBay Store)

Photo file storage:

- eBay>help>type: "Picture Manager overview"

Product Sourcing

eBay product sourcing, trending, and analysis:

- www.whatdoisell.com/studentrate

To find reputable wholesalers and liquidators:

- www.worldwidebrands.com/studentrate (Product Sourcing Membership)
- www.whatdoisell.com/studentrate

To find reputable drop shippers:

- www.worldwidebrands.com/studentrate (Product Sourcing Membership)

To find a manufacturer:

- www.thomasnet.com

To purchase wholesale on eBay:

- http://reseller.ebay.com/ns/home.html (for PowerSellers only)

For government surplus on eBay:

- http://pages.ebay.com/governmentsurplus/index.html

To find importers:

- www.globalsources.com
- www.worldwidebrands.com/studentrate (Product Sourcing Membership)

For importing research:

- www.globalsources.com
- www.importexporthelp.com
- http://globaledge.msu.edu
- www.busytrade.com
- www.rusbiz.com

Shipping

Free USPS/eBay co-branded Priority Mail boxes:

- http://ebaysupplies.usps.com

Corrugated boxes:

- www.uline.com

Packing supplies:

- www.uline.com
- www.papermart.com
- www.fast-pack.com
- www.ebay.com

Carriers:

- www.dhl.com 1-800-805-9306
- www.fedex.com 1-800-GoFedEx (1-800-463-3339)
- www.ups.com 1-800-PICK-UPS (1-800-742-5877)
- www.usps.com 1-800-ASK-USPS (1-800-275-8777)

Large item and freight carriers:

- www.freightquote.com
- www.uship.com
- www.dhl.com
- UPS Freight Service 1-800-333-7400
- www.fedex.com 1-800-GoFedEx (1-800-463-3339)

APO/FPO (military) shipping information:

- www.oconus.com/ZipCodes.asp

Private shipping insurance:

- www.u-pic.com
- www.dsiinsurance.com

UltraShip postal scales:

- www.trainingu4auctions.com
- www.trainingu4auctions.net (eBay Store)

Exporting:

- www.export.gov
- www.wcoomd.org
- www.export.gov/exportbasics
- www.sba.gov/aboutsba/sbaprograms/internationaltrade

Software Tools

Product analysis for eBay research:

- www.hammertap.com/studentrate

Niche and product analysis for Internet research:

- www.worldwidebrands.com/studentrate (instant market research, demand and competition research—all part of WWB's Product Sourcing Membership)

eBay auction management tools:

- eBay>site map>Turbo Lister
- eBay>site map>Blackthorne (and Blackthorne Pro)
- eBay>site map>Accounting Assistant
- eBay>site map>Sales Reports
- eBay>site map>Selling Manager

Third-party auction management tools (identified as web-based or desktop-based applications):

- Auction Hawk: www.auctionhawk.com (web)
- Auction Sage: www.auctionsagesoftware.com (desktop)
- Auction Wizard 2000: www.auctionwizard2000.com (desktop)
- ChannelAdvisor: www.channeladvisor.com (web)
- DEK Auction Manager: www.dekauctionmanager.com (desktop)

- Infopia: www.infopia.com (web)
- MarketplaceAdvisor (owned by ChannelAdvisor): www.channeladvisor.com/mw (web)
- Spoonfeeder: www.spoonfeeder.com (web)
- Vendio: www.vendio.com (web)
- Zoovy: www.zoovy.com (web)

Other Helpful Sites and Products

Computer-related help and tips:

- www.komando.com

eBay Seller Evaluation Checklist:

- www.trainingu4auctions.com

Escrow service:

- www.escrow.com

Foreign language translation software:

- www.freetranslation.com
- Google>Language (select the **Language** link)

Inexpensive logo design software:

- Logo Creator (electronics and office-supply stores)
- Logo Design (electronics and office-supply stores)

Interactive video for eBay listings:

- www.deal4it.com/studentrate

Inventions:

- www.legalzoom.com/studentrate (file patent)
- www.inventorsdigest.com
- www.alibaba.com (find manufacturers)

eBay Stores:

- www.ebay.com/stores

Videos on how to set up your store properly:

- www.StoresSuccessVideo.com/studentrate

Scams on eBay:

- www.millersmiles.co.uk/search/eBay
- Report spoof e-mails: spoof@ebay.com

Skype (eBay-owned Internet voice communication):

- www.skype.com

Trade shows:

- www.tsnn.com

U.S. Consumer Product Safety Commission (recalled products):

- www.cpsc.gov/cpscpub/prerel/prerel.html

Product Development Notebook

To download all worksheets and forms shown in this book free of charge:

- www.trainingu4auctions.com/notebook

The author's website and eBay Store for his students and readers (provides eBay buyer and seller tips, strategies, a newsletter, postal scales, and photography equipment):

- www.trainingu4auctions.com
- www.trainingu4auctions.net (eBay Store)

Other eBay books by this author:

- *eBay Rescue Problem Solver* (companion book to *eBay Rescue Profit Maker*; Alpha, 2009)
- *eBay Business at Your Fingertips* (Alpha, 2008)

Index